EDR Privileged Access Management Complete Self-Assessment Guide

The guidance in this Self-Assessment is based on EDR Privileged Access Management best practices and standards in business process architecture, design and quality management. The guidance is also based on the professional judgment of the individual collaborators listed in the Acknowledgments.

Notice of rights

You are licensed to use the Self-Assessment contents in your presentations and materials for internal use and customers without asking us - we are here to help.

All rights reserved for the book itself: this book may not be reproduced or transmitted in any form by any means, electronic, mechanical, photocopying, recording, or otherwise, without the prior written permission of the publisher.

The information in this book is distributed on an "As Is" basis without warranty. While every precaution has been taken in the preparation of he book, neither the author nor the publisher shall have any liability to any person or entity with respect to any loss or damage caused or alleged to be caused directly or indirectly by the instructions contained in this book or by the products described in it.

Trademarks

Many of the designations used by manufacturers and sellers to distinguish their products are claimed as trademarks. Where those designations appear in this book, and the publisher was aware of a trademark claim, the designations appear as requested by the owner of the trademark. All other product names and services identified throughout this book are used in editorial fashion only and for the benefit of such companies with no intention of infringement of the trademark. No such use, or the use of any trade name, is intended to convey endorsement or other affiliation with this book.

Copyright © by The Art of Service
http://theartofservice.com
service@theartofservice.com

Table of Contents

About The Art of Service

The Art of Service, Business Process Architects since 2000, is dedicated to helping stakeholders achieve excellence.

Defining, designing, creating, and implementing a process to solve a stakeholders challenge or meet an objective is the most valuable role… In EVERY group, company, organization and department.

Unless you're talking a one-time, single-use project, there should be a process. Whether that process is managed and implemented by humans, AI, or a combination of the two, it needs to be designed by someone with a complex enough perspective to ask the right questions.

Someone capable of asking the right questions and step back and say, 'What are we really trying to accomplish here? And is there a different way to look at it?'

With The Art of Service's Standard Requirements Self-Assessments, we empower people who can do just that — whether their title is marketer, entrepreneur, manager, salesperson, consultant, Business Process Manager, executive assistant, IT Manager, CIO etc... —they are the people who rule the future. They are people who watch the process as it happens, and ask the right questions to make the process work better.

Contact us when you need any support with this Self-Assessment and any help with templates, blue-prints and examples of standard documents you might need:

http://theartofservice.com
service@theartofservice.com

Acknowledgments

This checklist was developed under the auspices of The Art of Service, chaired by Gerardus Blokdyk.

Representatives from several client companies participated in the preparation of this Self-Assessment.

In addition, we are thankful for the design and printing services provided.

Included Resources - how to access

Included with your purchase of the book is the EDR Privileged Access Management Self-Assessment Spreadsheet Dashboard which contains all questions and Self-Assessment areas and auto-generates insights, graphs, and project RACI planning - all with examples to get you started right away.

How? Simply send an email to
access@theartofservice.com
with this books' title in the subject to get the EDR Privileged Access Management Self Assessment Tool right away.

You will receive the following contents with New and Updated specific criteria:

• The latest quick edition of the book in PDF

• The latest complete edition of the book in PDF, which criteria correspond to the criteria in...

• The Self-Assessment Excel Dashboard, and...

• Example pre-filled Self-Assessment Excel Dashboard to get familiar with results generation

• In-depth specific Checklists covering the topic

• Project management checklists and templates to assist with implementation

INCLUDES LIFETIME SELF ASSESSMENT UPDATES

Every self assessment comes with Lifetime Updates and Lifetime Free Updated Books. Lifetime Updates is an industry-first feature which allows you to receive verified self assessment updates, ensuring you always have the most accurate information at your fingertips.

Get it now- you will be glad you did - do it now, before you forget.

Send an email to **access@theartofservice.com** with this books' title in the subject to get the EDR Privileged Access Management Self Assessment Tool right away.

Your feedback is invaluable to us

If you recently bought this book, we would love to hear from you! You can do this by writing a review on amazon (or the online store where you purchased this book) about your last purchase! As part of our continual service improvement process, we love to hear real client experiences and feedback.

How does it work?
To post a review on Amazon, just log in to your account and click on the Create Your Own Review button (under Customer Reviews) of the relevant product page. You can find examples of product reviews in Amazon. If you purchased from another online store, simply follow their procedures.

What happens when I submit my review?
Once you have submitted your review, send us an email at review@theartofservice.com with the link to your review so we can properly thank you for your feedback.

Purpose of this Self-Assessment

This Self-Assessment has been developed to improve understanding of the requirements and elements of EDR Privileged Access Management, based on best practices and standards in business process architecture, design and quality management.

It is designed to allow for a rapid Self-Assessment to determine how closely existing management practices and procedures correspond to the elements of the Self-Assessment.

The criteria of requirements and elements of EDR Privileged Access Management have been rephrased in the format of a Self-Assessment questionnaire, with a seven-criterion scoring system, as explained in this document.

In this format, even with limited background knowledge of EDR Privileged Access Management, a manager can quickly review existing operations to determine how they measure up to the standards. This in turn can serve as the starting point of a 'gap analysis' to identify management tools or system elements that might usefully be implemented in the organization to help improve overall performance.

How to use the Self-Assessment

On the following pages are a series of questions to identify to what extent your EDR Privileged Access Management initiative is complete in comparison to the requirements set in standards.

To facilitate answering the questions, there is a space in front of each question to enter a score on a scale of '1' to '5'.

1 Strongly Disagree

2 Disagree

3 Neutral

4 Agree

5 Strongly Agree

Read the question and rate it with the following in front of mind:

'In my belief, the answer to this question is clearly defined'.

There are two ways in which you can choose to interpret this statement;
1. how aware are you that the answer to the question is clearly defined

2. for more in-depth analysis you can choose to gather evidence and confirm the answer to the question. This obviously will take more time, most Self-Assessment users opt for the first way to interpret the question and dig deeper later on based on the outcome of the overall Self-Assessment.

A score of '1' would mean that the answer is not clear at all, where a '5' would mean the answer is crystal clear and defined. Leave emtpy when the question is not applicable or you don't want to answer it, you can skip it without affecting your score. Write your score in the space provided.

After you have responded to all the appropriate statements in each section, compute your average score for that section, using the formula provided, and round to the nearest tenth. Then transfer to the corresponding spoke in the EDR Privileged Access Management Scorecard on the second next page of the Self-Assessment.

Your completed EDR Privileged Access Management Scorecard will give you a clear presentation of which EDR Privileged Access Management areas need attention.

EDR Privileged Access Management Scorecard Example

Example of how the finalized Scorecard can look like:

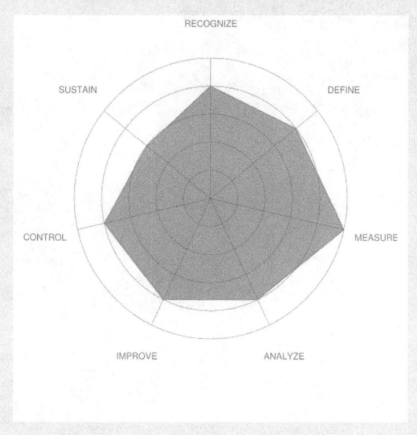

EDR Privileged Access Management Scorecard

Your Scores:

BEGINNING OF THE SELF-ASSESSMENT:

CRITERION #1: RECOGNIZE

INTENT: Be aware of the need for change. Recognize that there is an unfavorable variation, problem or symptom.

In my belief, the answer to this question is clearly defined:

5 Strongly Agree

4 Agree

3 Neutral

2 Disagree

1 Strongly Disagree

1. Who needs to know?
<--- Score

2. Does your organization need more EDR privileged access management education?
<--- Score

3. Are there any revenue recognition issues?
<--- Score

4. Who defines the rules in relation to any given issue?
<--- Score

5. What are the timeframes required to resolve each of the issues/problems?
<--- Score

6. What situation(s) led to this EDR privileged access management Self Assessment?
<--- Score

7. How do you recognize an objection?
<--- Score

8. What is the problem or issue?
<--- Score

9. For your EDR privileged access management project, identify and describe the business environment, is there more than one layer to the business environment?
<--- Score

10. How much are sponsors, customers, partners, stakeholders involved in EDR privileged access management? In other words, what are the risks, if EDR privileged access management does not deliver successfully?
<--- Score

11. Will it solve real problems?
<--- Score

12. Who needs what information?
<--- Score

13. Who should resolve the EDR privileged access management issues?
<--- Score

14. To what extent does each concerned units management team recognize EDR privileged access management as an effective investment?
<--- Score

15. How can auditing be a preventative security measure?
<--- Score

16. What do you need to start doing?
<--- Score

17. Where do you need to exercise leadership?
<--- Score

18. How are training requirements identified?
<--- Score

19. Are you dealing with any of the same issues today as yesterday? What can you do about this?
<--- Score

20. What does EDR privileged access management success mean to the stakeholders?
<--- Score

21. Are there EDR privileged access management problems defined?
<--- Score

22. Are your goals realistic? Do you need to

redefine your problem? Perhaps the problem has changed or maybe you have reached your goal and need to set a new one?
<--- Score

23. How many trainings, in total, are needed?
<--- Score

24. Are there recognized EDR privileged access management problems?
<--- Score

25. What EDR privileged access management problem should be solved?
<--- Score

26. Can management personnel recognize the monetary benefit of EDR privileged access management?
<--- Score

27. What are the stakeholder objectives to be achieved with EDR privileged access management?
<--- Score

28. What resources or support might you need?
<--- Score

29. Why the need?
<--- Score

30. Are employees recognized or rewarded for performance that demonstrates the highest levels of integrity?
<--- Score

31. Have you identified your EDR privileged access management key performance indicators?
<--- Score

32. What needs to stay?
<--- Score

33. What EDR privileged access management coordination do you need?
<--- Score

34. Does EDR privileged access management create potential expectations in other areas that need to be recognized and considered?
<--- Score

35. How are the EDR privileged access management's objectives aligned to the group's overall stakeholder strategy?
<--- Score

36. Are there any specific expectations or concerns about the EDR privileged access management team, EDR privileged access management itself?
<--- Score

37. What is the smallest subset of the problem you can usefully solve?
<--- Score

38. How are you going to measure success?
<--- Score

39. What is the extent or complexity of the EDR privileged access management problem?
<--- Score

40. What needs to be done?
<--- Score

41. What information do users need?
<--- Score

42. Are losses recognized in a timely manner?
<--- Score

43. Do you need different information or graphics?
<--- Score

44. What is the EDR privileged access management problem definition? What do you need to resolve?
<--- Score

45. What are the clients issues and concerns?
<--- Score

46. Do you have/need 24-hour access to key personnel?
<--- Score

47. What would happen if EDR privileged access management weren't done?
<--- Score

48. Does the problem have ethical dimensions?
<--- Score

49. What vendors make products that address the EDR privileged access management needs?
<--- Score

50. Did you miss any major EDR privileged access

management issues?
<--- Score

51. Think about the people you identified for your EDR privileged access management project and the project responsibilities you would assign to them, what kind of training do you think they would need to perform these responsibilities effectively?
<--- Score

52. What training and capacity building actions are needed to implement proposed reforms?
<--- Score

53. What are the expected benefits of EDR privileged access management to the stakeholder?
<--- Score

54. What extra resources will you need?
<--- Score

55. To what extent would your organization benefit from being recognized as a award recipient?
<--- Score

56. What prevents you from making the changes you know will make you a more effective EDR privileged access management leader?
<--- Score

57. Who needs to know about EDR privileged access management?
<--- Score

58. Why is this needed?

<--- Score

59. Which issues are too important to ignore?
<--- Score

60. What should be considered when identifying available resources, constraints, and deadlines?
<--- Score

61. Is the need for organizational change recognized?
<--- Score

62. As a sponsor, customer or management, how important is it to meet goals, objectives?
<--- Score

63. Which needs are not included or involved?
<--- Score

64. Are employees recognized for desired behaviors?
<--- Score

65. Is it clear when you think of the day ahead of you what activities and tasks you need to complete?
<--- Score

66. How do you identify subcontractor relationships?
<--- Score

67. Is the quality assurance team identified?
<--- Score

68. Who needs budgets?
<--- Score

69. Are problem definition and motivation clearly presented?
<--- Score

70. How do you recognize an EDR privileged access management objection?
<--- Score

71. What is the recognized need?
<--- Score

72. Who are your key stakeholders who need to sign off?
<--- Score

73. What activities does the governance board need to consider?
<--- Score

74. What do employees need in the short term?
<--- Score

75. What are the minority interests and what amount of minority interests can be recognized?
<--- Score

76. Are controls defined to recognize and contain problems?
<--- Score

77. How do you identify the kinds of information that you will need?
<--- Score

78. What problems are you facing and how do you consider EDR privileged access management will

circumvent those obstacles?
<--- Score

79. Where is training needed?
<--- Score

80. What else needs to be measured?
<--- Score

81. Do you recognize EDR privileged access management achievements?
<--- Score

82. How do you take a forward-looking perspective in identifying EDR privileged access management research related to market response and models?
<--- Score

83. How does it fit into your organizational needs and tasks?
<--- Score

84. What are the EDR privileged access management resources needed?
<--- Score

85. Which information does the EDR privileged access management business case need to include?
<--- Score

86. What is the problem and/or vulnerability?
<--- Score

87. What EDR privileged access management events should you attend?

<--- Score

88. Is it needed?
<--- Score

89. Do you need to avoid or amend any EDR privileged access management activities?
<--- Score

90. What are your needs in relation to EDR privileged access management skills, labor, equipment, and markets?
<--- Score

91. Who else hopes to benefit from it?
<--- Score

92. Looking at each person individually – does every one have the qualities which are needed to work in this group?
<--- Score

93. What EDR privileged access management capabilities do you need?
<--- Score

94. What tools and technologies are needed for a custom EDR privileged access management project?
<--- Score

95. Are there regulatory / compliance issues?
<--- Score

96. How do you assess your EDR privileged access management workforce capability and capacity needs, including skills, competencies, and staffing

levels?
<--- Score

97. Will EDR privileged access management deliverables need to be tested and, if so, by whom?
<--- Score

98. Do you know what you need to know about EDR privileged access management?
<--- Score

Add up total points for this section:
_ _ _ _ _ = Total points for this section

Divided by: _ _ _ _ _ _ (number of statements answered) = _ _ _ _ _ _
Average score for this section

Transfer your score to the EDR privileged access management Index at the beginning of the Self-Assessment.

CRITERION #2: DEFINE:

INTENT: Formulate the stakeholder problem. Define the problem, needs and objectives.

In my belief, the answer to this question is clearly defined:

5 Strongly Agree

4 Agree

3 Neutral

2 Disagree

1 Strongly Disagree

1. What sources do you use to gather information for a EDR privileged access management study?
<--- Score

2. What are the record-keeping requirements of EDR privileged access management activities?
<--- Score

3. How and when will the baselines be defined?

<--- Score

4. Has a high-level 'as is' process map been completed, verified and validated?
<--- Score

5. What happens if EDR privileged access management's scope changes?
<--- Score

6. How do you think the partners involved in EDR privileged access management would have defined success?
<--- Score

7. Scope of sensitive information?
<--- Score

8. What are the Roles and Responsibilities for each team member and its leadership? Where is this documented?
<--- Score

9. Is the work to date meeting requirements?
<--- Score

10. Is there a EDR privileged access management management charter, including stakeholder case, problem and goal statements, scope, milestones, roles and responsibilities, communication plan?
<--- Score

11. Who are the EDR privileged access management improvement team members, including Management Leads and Coaches?
<--- Score

12. What would be the goal or target for a EDR privileged access management's improvement team?
<--- Score

13. Do you have organizational privacy requirements?
<--- Score

14. How did the EDR privileged access management manager receive input to the development of a EDR privileged access management improvement plan and the estimated completion dates/times of each activity?
<--- Score

15. What sort of initial information to gather?
<--- Score

16. What is the definition of success?
<--- Score

17. Where can you gather more information?
<--- Score

18. Do you all define EDR privileged access management in the same way?
<--- Score

19. Are there different segments of customers?
<--- Score

20. Who is gathering information?
<--- Score

21. What is the scope of the EDR privileged access management work?

<--- Score

22. What knowledge or experience is required?
<--- Score

23. What gets examined?
<--- Score

24. The political context: who holds power?
<--- Score

25. Are task requirements clearly defined?
<--- Score

26. How do you gather the stories?
<--- Score

27. Are roles and responsibilities formally defined?
<--- Score

28. What EDR privileged access management requirements should be gathered?
<--- Score

29. How will the EDR privileged access management team and the group measure complete success of EDR privileged access management?
<--- Score

30. Are all requirements met?
<--- Score

31. Are there any constraints known that bear on the ability to perform EDR privileged access management work? How is the team addressing them?
<--- Score

32. Is there a critical path to deliver EDR privileged access management results?
<--- Score

33. Has everyone on the team, including the team leaders, been properly trained?
<--- Score

34. Does the scope remain the same?
<--- Score

35. What scope to assess?
<--- Score

36. How does the EDR privileged access management manager ensure against scope creep?
<--- Score

37. What are the dynamics of the communication plan?
<--- Score

38. Are required metrics defined, what are they?
<--- Score

39. In what way can you redefine the criteria of choice clients have in your category in your favor?
<--- Score

40. How are consistent EDR privileged access management definitions important?
<--- Score

41. What information should you gather?
<--- Score

42. Are the EDR privileged access management requirements complete?

<--- Score

43. Is EDR privileged access management required?

<--- Score

44. What baselines are required to be defined and managed?

<--- Score

45. What critical content must be communicated – who, what, when, where, and how?

<--- Score

46. What are (control) requirements for EDR privileged access management Information?

<--- Score

47. How do you build the right business case?

<--- Score

48. Will team members regularly document their EDR privileged access management work?

<--- Score

49. What are the compelling stakeholder reasons for embarking on EDR privileged access management?

<--- Score

50. Are accountability and ownership for EDR privileged access management clearly defined?

<--- Score

51. Have the customer needs been translated into specific, measurable requirements? How?
<--- Score

52. How is the team tracking and documenting its work?
<--- Score

53. Is the EDR privileged access management scope complete and appropriately sized?
<--- Score

54. Will team members perform EDR privileged access management work when assigned and in a timely fashion?
<--- Score

55. What constraints exist that might impact the team?
<--- Score

56. Is special EDR privileged access management user knowledge required?
<--- Score

57. Is there a completed SIPOC representation, describing the Suppliers, Inputs, Process, Outputs, and Customers?
<--- Score

58. How often are the team meetings?
<--- Score

59. Is there a clear EDR privileged access management case definition?
<--- Score

60. Has the improvement team collected the 'voice of the customer' (obtained feedback – qualitative and quantitative)?
<--- Score

61. Are customer(s) identified and segmented according to their different needs and requirements?
<--- Score

62. What intelligence can you gather?
<--- Score

63. Is the team adequately staffed with the desired cross-functionality? If not, what additional resources are available to the team?
<--- Score

64. Is EDR privileged access management currently on schedule according to the plan?
<--- Score

65. Is there any additional EDR privileged access management definition of success?
<--- Score

66. What is the definition of EDR privileged access management excellence?
<--- Score

67. What defines best in class?
<--- Score

68. Why are you doing EDR privileged access management and what is the scope?
<--- Score

69. What are the EDR privileged access management use cases?
<--- Score

70. Has anyone else (internal or external to the group) attempted to solve this problem or a similar one before? If so, what knowledge can be leveraged from these previous efforts?
<--- Score

71. What scope do you want your strategy to cover?
<--- Score

72. What is the worst case scenario?
<--- Score

73. How do you gather requirements?
<--- Score

74. What specifically is the problem? Where does it occur? When does it occur? What is its extent?
<--- Score

75. Has the direction changed at all during the course of EDR privileged access management? If so, when did it change and why?
<--- Score

76. Have all basic functions of EDR privileged access management been defined?
<--- Score

77. How do you keep key subject matter experts in the loop?
<--- Score

78. Is the current 'as is' process being followed? If not, what are the discrepancies?
<--- Score

79. Has a EDR privileged access management requirement not been met?
<--- Score

80. When is/was the EDR privileged access management start date?
<--- Score

81. What are the requirements for audit information?
<--- Score

82. Who approved the EDR privileged access management scope?
<--- Score

83. Have specific policy objectives been defined?
<--- Score

84. Has/have the customer(s) been identified?
<--- Score

85. How will variation in the actual durations of each activity be dealt with to ensure that the expected EDR privileged access management results are met?
<--- Score

86. What is out-of-scope initially?
<--- Score

87. Who is gathering EDR privileged access management information?

<--- Score

88. Who defines (or who defined) the rules and roles?
<--- Score

89. How do you catch EDR privileged access management definition inconsistencies?
<--- Score

90. Is there a completed, verified, and validated high-level 'as is' (not 'should be' or 'could be') stakeholder process map?
<--- Score

91. What is a worst-case scenario for losses?
<--- Score

92. Is the team equipped with available and reliable resources?
<--- Score

93. Has the EDR privileged access management work been fairly and/or equitably divided and delegated among team members who are qualified and capable to perform the work? Has everyone contributed?
<--- Score

94. How was the 'as is' process map developed, reviewed, verified and validated?
<--- Score

95. When are meeting minutes sent out? Who is on the distribution list?
<--- Score

96. Has your scope been defined?
<--- Score

97. Have all of the relationships been defined properly?
<--- Score

98. Do the problem and goal statements meet the SMART criteria (specific, measurable, attainable, relevant, and time-bound)?
<--- Score

99. What is in scope?
<--- Score

100. Is it clearly defined in and to your organization what you do?
<--- Score

101. Will a EDR privileged access management production readiness review be required?
<--- Score

102. Is EDR privileged access management linked to key stakeholder goals and objectives?
<--- Score

103. Is the EDR privileged access management scope manageable?
<--- Score

104. What is the scope of EDR privileged access management?
<--- Score

105. Are audit criteria, scope, frequency and methods

defined?

<--- Score

106. Is the improvement team aware of the different versions of a process: what they think it is vs. what it actually is vs. what it should be vs. what it could be?

<--- Score

107. How would you define EDR privileged access management leadership?

<--- Score

108. How do you manage scope?

<--- Score

109. Has a project plan, Gantt chart, or similar been developed/completed?

<--- Score

110. What is the context?

<--- Score

111. What are the boundaries of the scope? What is in bounds and what is not? What is the start point? What is the stop point?

<--- Score

112. Are different versions of process maps needed to account for the different types of inputs?

<--- Score

113. Has a team charter been developed and communicated?

<--- Score

114. What key stakeholder process output measure(s)

does EDR privileged access management leverage and how?
<--- Score

115. What is the scope of the EDR privileged access management effort?
<--- Score

116. What system do you use for gathering EDR privileged access management information?
<--- Score

117. What are the tasks and definitions?
<--- Score

118. When is the estimated completion date?
<--- Score

119. Is data collected and displayed to better understand customer(s) critical needs and requirements.
<--- Score

120. What was the context?
<--- Score

121. Is there regularly 100% attendance at the team meetings? If not, have appointed substitutes attended to preserve cross-functionality and full representation?
<--- Score

122. Are approval levels defined for contracts and supplements to contracts?
<--- Score

123. Are the EDR privileged access management requirements testable?
<--- Score

124. How do you gather EDR privileged access management requirements?
<--- Score

125. Does the team have regular meetings?
<--- Score

126. What are the core elements of the EDR privileged access management business case?
<--- Score

127. Is the scope of EDR privileged access management defined?
<--- Score

128. What are the rough order estimates on cost savings/opportunities that EDR privileged access management brings?
<--- Score

129. How can the value of EDR privileged access management be defined?
<--- Score

130. How do you manage unclear EDR privileged access management requirements?
<--- Score

131. If substitutes have been appointed, have they been briefed on the EDR privileged access management goals and received regular communications as to the progress to date?

<--- Score

132. What EDR privileged access management
services do you require?
<--- Score

133. How do you manage changes in EDR privileged
access management requirements?
<--- Score

134. What is in the scope and what is not in scope?
<--- Score

135. What customer feedback methods were used to
solicit their input?
<--- Score

136. What is out of scope?
<--- Score

Add up total points for this section:
_ _ _ _ _ = Total points for this section

Divided by: _ _ _ _ _ _ (number of
statements answered) = _ _ _ _ _ _
Average score for this section

Transfer your score to the EDR
privileged access management Index at
the beginning of the Self-Assessment.

CRITERION #3: MEASURE:

INTENT: Gather the correct data.
Measure the current performance and
evolution of the situation.

In my belief, the answer to this
question is clearly defined:

5 Strongly Agree

4 Agree

3 Neutral

2 Disagree

1 Strongly Disagree

1. How is performance measured?
<--- Score

2. What relevant entities could be measured?
<--- Score

3. Are the units of measure consistent?
<--- Score

4. What are the costs of reform?
<--- Score

5. What is your EDR privileged access management quality cost segregation study?
<--- Score

6. Who should receive measurement reports?
<--- Score

7. What are hidden EDR privileged access management quality costs?
<--- Score

8. What are your operating costs?
<--- Score

9. Does management have the right priorities among projects?
<--- Score

10. How can you reduce the costs of obtaining inputs?
<--- Score

11. How is the value delivered by EDR privileged access management being measured?
<--- Score

12. What are the costs of delaying EDR privileged access management action?
<--- Score

13. How are measurements made?
<--- Score

14. Which costs should be taken into account?

<--- Score

15. What potential environmental factors impact the EDR privileged access management effort?
<--- Score

16. What does losing customers cost your organization?
<--- Score

17. Have you included everything in your EDR privileged access management cost models?
<--- Score

18. What are the uncertainties surrounding estimates of impact?
<--- Score

19. Are the EDR privileged access management benefits worth its costs?
<--- Score

20. Is there an opportunity to verify requirements?
<--- Score

21. What are the types and number of measures to use?
<--- Score

22. What methods are feasible and acceptable to estimate the impact of reforms?
<--- Score

23. What is the root cause(s) of the problem?
<--- Score

24. Are you able to realize any cost savings?
<--- Score

25. What are the EDR privileged access management investment costs?
<--- Score

26. How do you verify performance?
<--- Score

27. What is the cause of any EDR privileged access management gaps?
<--- Score

28. What are the strategic priorities for this year?
<--- Score

29. What measurements are possible, practicable and meaningful?
<--- Score

30. What is the EDR privileged access management business impact?
<--- Score

31. How will measures be used to manage and adapt?
<--- Score

32. How do you verify and develop ideas and innovations?
<--- Score

33. What is the total fixed cost?
<--- Score

34. What tests verify requirements?

<--- Score

35. Are actual costs in line with budgeted costs?
<--- Score

36. What causes extra work or rework?
<--- Score

37. How much does it cost?
<--- Score

38. Which measures and indicators matter?
<--- Score

39. How do you verify the EDR privileged access management requirements quality?
<--- Score

40. When a disaster occurs, who gets priority?
<--- Score

41. How do your measurements capture actionable EDR privileged access management information for use in exceeding your customers expectations and securing your customers engagement?
<--- Score

42. What are your primary costs, revenues, assets?
<--- Score

43. What causes innovation to fail or succeed in your organization?
<--- Score

44. What would it cost to replace your technology?
<--- Score

45. How do you verify if EDR privileged access management is built right?
<--- Score

46. Are you aware of what could cause a problem?
<--- Score

47. How will you measure success?
<--- Score

48. Are the measurements objective?
<--- Score

49. What is your decision requirements diagram?
<--- Score

50. Is the solution cost-effective?
<--- Score

51. Does the EDR privileged access management task fit the client's priorities?
<--- Score

52. Why do the measurements/indicators matter?
<--- Score

53. How will costs be allocated?
<--- Score

54. How do you aggregate measures across priorities?
<--- Score

55. How can you measure EDR privileged access management in a systematic way?
<--- Score

56. How do you verify your resources?
<--- Score

57. How long to keep data and how to manage retention costs?
<--- Score

58. What is the cost of rework?
<--- Score

59. What are the EDR privileged access management key cost drivers?
<--- Score

60. Where is it measured?
<--- Score

61. Do you have an issue in getting priority?
<--- Score

62. What are the operational costs after EDR privileged access management deployment?
<--- Score

63. What is measured? Why?
<--- Score

64. What happens if cost savings do not materialize?
<--- Score

65. How do you measure variability?
<--- Score

66. Are indirect costs charged to the EDR

privileged access management program?
<--- Score

67. Has a cost center been established?
<--- Score

68. What does your operating model cost?
<--- Score

69. Will EDR privileged access management have an impact on current business continuity, disaster recovery processes and/or infrastructure?
<--- Score

70. Have you made assumptions about the shape of the future, particularly its impact on your customers and competitors?
<--- Score

71. Are there measurements based on task performance?
<--- Score

72. How can you manage cost down?
<--- Score

73. How are costs allocated?
<--- Score

74. Is the cost worth the EDR privileged access management effort ?
<--- Score

75. What would be a real cause for concern?
<--- Score

76. Do you have a flow diagram of what happens?
<--- Score

77. How can you measure the performance?
<--- Score

78. Do the benefits outweigh the costs?
<--- Score

79. Why do you expend time and effort to implement measurement, for whom?
<--- Score

80. When are costs are incurred?
<--- Score

81. How can you reduce costs?
<--- Score

82. How will your organization measure success?
<--- Score

83. Are supply costs steady or fluctuating?
<--- Score

84. What are the costs and benefits?
<--- Score

85. How will effects be measured?
<--- Score

86. What could cause you to change course?
<--- Score

87. Are EDR privileged access management vulnerabilities categorized and prioritized?

<--- Score

88. What are the current costs of the EDR privileged access management process?
<--- Score

89. How will you measure your EDR privileged access management effectiveness?
<--- Score

90. How do you measure efficient delivery of EDR privileged access management services?
<--- Score

91. What are the costs?
<--- Score

92. Do you aggressively reward and promote the people who have the biggest impact on creating excellent EDR privileged access management services/products?
<--- Score

93. What do people want to verify?
<--- Score

94. What is the total cost related to deploying EDR privileged access management, including any consulting or professional services?
<--- Score

95. What are allowable costs?
<--- Score

96. What does a Test Case verify?
<--- Score

97. Are you taking your company in the direction of better and revenue or cheaper and cost?
<--- Score

98. Who pays the cost?
<--- Score

99. How will success or failure be measured?
<--- Score

100. Is it possible to estimate the impact of unanticipated complexity such as wrong or failed assumptions, feedback, etcetera on proposed reforms?
<--- Score

101. What causes mismanagement?
<--- Score

102. What do you measure and why?
<--- Score

103. Have design-to-cost goals been established?
<--- Score

104. Was a business case (cost/benefit) developed?
<--- Score

105. How do you prevent mis-estimating cost?
<--- Score

106. Do you effectively measure and reward individual and team performance?
<--- Score

107. What evidence is there and what is measured?
<--- Score

108. What is an unallowable cost?
<--- Score

109. What are the estimated costs of proposed changes?
<--- Score

110. How do you measure success?
<--- Score

111. What can be used to verify compliance?
<--- Score

112. What drives O&M cost?
<--- Score

113. Did you tackle the cause or the symptom?
<--- Score

114. How do you control the overall costs of your work processes?
<--- Score

115. How can a EDR privileged access management test verify your ideas or assumptions?
<--- Score

116. When should you bother with diagrams?
<--- Score

117. What measurements are being captured?
<--- Score

118. At what cost?
<--- Score

119. How do you measure lifecycle phases?
<--- Score

120. Do you have any cost EDR privileged access management limitation requirements?
<--- Score

121. How sensitive must the EDR privileged access management strategy be to cost?
<--- Score

122. How do you quantify and qualify impacts?
<--- Score

123. Among the EDR privileged access management product and service cost to be estimated, which is considered hardest to estimate?
<--- Score

124. How is progress measured?
<--- Score

125. How to cause the change?
<--- Score

126. Are there competing EDR privileged access management priorities?
<--- Score

127. What could cause delays in the schedule?
<--- Score

128. Are there any easy-to-implement alternatives

to EDR privileged access management? Sometimes other solutions are available that do not require the cost implications of a full-blown project?
<--- Score

129. Are missed EDR privileged access management opportunities costing your organization money?
<--- Score

130. What harm might be caused?
<--- Score

131. Which EDR privileged access management impacts are significant?
<--- Score

Add up total points for this section:
_ _ _ _ _ = Total points for this section

Divided by: _ _ _ _ _ _ (number of statements answered) = _ _ _ _ _ _
Average score for this section

Transfer your score to the EDR privileged access management Index at the beginning of the Self-Assessment.

CRITERION #4: ANALYZE:

INTENT: Analyze causes, assumptions and hypotheses.

In my belief, the answer to this question is clearly defined:

5 Strongly Agree

4 Agree

3 Neutral

2 Disagree

1 Strongly Disagree

1. What are your outputs?
<--- Score

2. What are the disruptive EDR privileged access management technologies that enable your organization to radically change your business processes?
<--- Score

3. Are your outputs consistent?

<--- Score

4. How has the EDR privileged access management data been gathered?
<--- Score

5. Do quality systems drive continuous improvement?
<--- Score

6. What is the output?
<--- Score

7. What are the revised rough estimates of the financial savings/opportunity for EDR privileged access management improvements?
<--- Score

8. Is the required EDR privileged access management data gathered?
<--- Score

9. Were any designed experiments used to generate additional insight into the data analysis?
<--- Score

10. Are EDR privileged access management changes recognized early enough to be approved through the regular process?
<--- Score

11. Who is involved with workflow mapping?
<--- Score

12. How do you ensure that the EDR privileged access management opportunity is realistic?
<--- Score

13. Record-keeping requirements flow from the records needed as inputs, outputs, controls and for transformation of a EDR privileged access management process, are the records needed as inputs to the EDR privileged access management process available?
<--- Score

14. How do you define collaboration and team output?
<--- Score

15. Who gets your output?
<--- Score

16. Where can you get qualified talent today?
<--- Score

17. What other jobs or tasks affect the performance of the steps in the EDR privileged access management process?
<--- Score

18. Do your leaders quickly bounce back from setbacks?
<--- Score

19. What is the complexity of the output produced?
<--- Score

20. What are the EDR privileged access management design outputs?
<--- Score

21. What are the personnel training and qualifications

required?

<--- Score

22. What output to create?

<--- Score

23. What EDR privileged access management data should be collected?

<--- Score

24. What do you need to qualify?

<--- Score

25. What tools were used to narrow the list of possible causes?

<--- Score

26. Do several people in different organizational units assist with the EDR privileged access management process?

<--- Score

27. What internal processes need improvement?

<--- Score

28. Are all team members qualified for all tasks?

<--- Score

29. What qualifications are needed?

<--- Score

30. Has data output been validated?

<--- Score

31. How is the way you as the leader think and process information affecting your organizational

culture?
<--- Score

32. An organizationally feasible system request is one that considers the mission, goals and objectives of the organization, key questions are: is the EDR privileged access management solution request practical and will it solve a problem or take advantage of an opportunity to achieve company goals?
<--- Score

33. What were the crucial 'moments of truth' on the process map?
<--- Score

34. Was a detailed process map created to amplify critical steps of the 'as is' stakeholder process?
<--- Score

35. What are the necessary qualifications?
<--- Score

36. What is your organizations system for selecting qualified vendors?
<--- Score

37. How do your work systems and key work processes relate to and capitalize on your core competencies?
<--- Score

38. Are you missing EDR privileged access management opportunities?
<--- Score

39. How will the EDR privileged access management

data be captured?

<--- Score

40. What other organizational variables, such as reward systems or communication systems, affect the performance of this EDR privileged access management process?

<--- Score

41. What are your current levels and trends in key measures or indicators of EDR privileged access management product and process performance that are important to and directly serve your customers? How do these results compare with the performance of your competitors and other organizations with similar offerings?

<--- Score

42. Is there a strict change management process?

<--- Score

43. What controls do you have in place to protect data?

<--- Score

44. What are your best practices for minimizing EDR privileged access management project risk, while demonstrating incremental value and quick wins throughout the EDR privileged access management project lifecycle?

<--- Score

45. Do staff qualifications match your project?

<--- Score

46. What is the Value Stream Mapping?

<--- Score

47. Did any value-added analysis or 'lean thinking' take place to identify some of the gaps shown on the 'as is' process map?
<--- Score

48. Were Pareto charts (or similar) used to portray the 'heavy hitters' (or key sources of variation)?
<--- Score

49. What EDR privileged access management data do you gather or use now?
<--- Score

50. What kind of crime could a potential new hire have committed that would not only not disqualify him/her from being hired by your organization, but would actually indicate that he/she might be a particularly good fit?
<--- Score

51. What are your current levels and trends in key EDR privileged access management measures or indicators of product and process performance that are important to and directly serve your customers?
<--- Score

52. Who qualifies to gain access to data?
<--- Score

53. What data do you need to collect?
<--- Score

54. What is the cost of poor quality as supported by

the team's analysis?
<--- Score

55. How are outputs preserved and protected?
<--- Score

56. How do you promote understanding that opportunity for improvement is not criticism of the status quo, or the people who created the status quo?
<--- Score

57. How will the data be checked for quality?
<--- Score

58. How can risk management be tied procedurally to process elements?
<--- Score

59. Were there any improvement opportunities identified from the process analysis?
<--- Score

60. How does the organization define, manage, and improve its EDR privileged access management processes?
<--- Score

61. Have any additional benefits been identified that will result from closing all or most of the gaps?
<--- Score

62. What are your EDR privileged access management processes?
<--- Score

63. Where is EDR privileged access management data gathered?
<--- Score

64. Is the final output clearly identified?
<--- Score

65. What training and qualifications will you need?
<--- Score

66. Have the problem and goal statements been updated to reflect the additional knowledge gained from the analyze phase?
<--- Score

67. What systems/processes must you excel at?
<--- Score

68. Is data and process analysis, root cause analysis and quantifying the gap/opportunity in place?
<--- Score

69. How is EDR privileged access management data gathered?
<--- Score

70. Has an output goal been set?
<--- Score

71. What methods do you use to gather EDR privileged access management data?
<--- Score

72. Is there an established change management process?
<--- Score

73. What qualifications and skills do you need?
<--- Score

74. Have you defined which data is gathered how?
<--- Score

75. What data is gathered?
<--- Score

76. Do your employees have the opportunity to do what they do best everyday?
<--- Score

77. What are evaluation criteria for the output?
<--- Score

78. How do you identify specific EDR privileged access management investment opportunities and emerging trends?
<--- Score

79. What are the processes for audit reporting and management?
<--- Score

80. What resources go in to get the desired output?
<--- Score

81. What are your key performance measures or indicators and in-process measures for the control and improvement of your EDR privileged access management processes?
<--- Score

82. What are the best opportunities for value

improvement?

<--- Score

83. Think about the functions involved in your EDR privileged access management project, what processes flow from these functions?

<--- Score

84. How difficult is it to qualify what EDR privileged access management ROI is?

<--- Score

85. Which EDR privileged access management data should be retained?

<--- Score

86. What qualifications do EDR privileged access management leaders need?

<--- Score

87. Who owns what data?

<--- Score

88. Who is involved in the management review process?

<--- Score

89. Are all staff in core EDR privileged access management subjects Highly Qualified?

<--- Score

90. What process should you select for improvement?

<--- Score

91. What does the data say about the performance of the stakeholder process?

<--- Score

92. How was the detailed process map generated, verified, and validated?
<--- Score

93. Is there any way to speed up the process?
<--- Score

94. Did any additional data need to be collected?
<--- Score

95. A compounding model resolution with available relevant data can often provide insight towards a solution methodology; which EDR privileged access management models, tools and techniques are necessary?
<--- Score

96. How do you implement and manage your work processes to ensure that they meet design requirements?
<--- Score

97. Who will gather what data?
<--- Score

98. How much data can be collected in the given timeframe?
<--- Score

99. What process improvements will be needed?
<--- Score

100. How will the change process be managed?
<--- Score

101. Should you invest in industry-recognized qualifications?

<--- Score

102. How is the data gathered?

<--- Score

103. What qualifications are necessary?

<--- Score

104. How do you measure the operational performance of your key work systems and processes, including productivity, cycle time, and other appropriate measures of process effectiveness, efficiency, and innovation?

<--- Score

105. Is the suppliers process defined and controlled?

<--- Score

106. Is the gap/opportunity displayed and communicated in financial terms?

<--- Score

107. What tools were used to generate the list of possible causes?

<--- Score

108. Is the performance gap determined?

<--- Score

109. Do your contracts/agreements contain data security obligations?

<--- Score

110. How is the EDR privileged access management Value Stream Mapping managed?

<--- Score

111. Do you understand your management processes today?

<--- Score

112. What types of data do your EDR privileged access management indicators require?

<--- Score

113. Think about some of the processes you undertake within your organization, which do you own?

<--- Score

114. Can you add value to the current EDR privileged access management decision-making process (largely qualitative) by incorporating uncertainty modeling (more quantitative)?

<--- Score

115. Do you, as a leader, bounce back quickly from setbacks?

<--- Score

116. What are the EDR privileged access management business drivers?

<--- Score

117. Where is the data coming from to measure compliance?

<--- Score

118. What did the team gain from developing a sub-

process map?
<--- Score

119. What EDR privileged access management data should be managed?
<--- Score

120. What, related to, EDR privileged access management processes does your organization outsource?
<--- Score

121. What EDR privileged access management data will be collected?
<--- Score

122. Is the EDR privileged access management process severely broken such that a re-design is necessary?
<--- Score

123. Is pre-qualification of suppliers carried out?
<--- Score

124. What is the EDR privileged access management Driver?
<--- Score

125. Who will facilitate the team and process?
<--- Score

126. What were the financial benefits resulting from any 'ground fruit or low-hanging fruit' (quick fixes)?
<--- Score

127. What conclusions were drawn from the team's

data collection and analysis? How did the team reach these conclusions?
<--- Score

128. Identify an operational issue in your organization, for example, could a particular task be done more quickly or more efficiently by EDR privileged access management?
<--- Score

129. What quality tools were used to get through the analyze phase?
<--- Score

130. What is the oversight process?
<--- Score

131. What will drive EDR privileged access management change?
<--- Score

132. What information qualified as important?
<--- Score

133. Was a cause-and-effect diagram used to explore the different types of causes (or sources of variation)?
<--- Score

134. What EDR privileged access management metrics are outputs of the process?
<--- Score

135. How many input/output points does it require?
<--- Score

Add up total points for this section:
_____ = Total points for this section

Divided by: _____ (number of
statements answered) = _____
Average score for this section

Transfer your score to the EDR
privileged access management Index at
the beginning of the Self-Assessment.

CRITERION #5: IMPROVE:

INTENT: Develop a practical solution. Innovate, establish and test the solution and to measure the results.

In my belief, the answer to this question is clearly defined:

5 Strongly Agree

4 Agree

3 Neutral

2 Disagree

1 Strongly Disagree

1. Risk events: what are the things that could go wrong?
<--- Score

2. What are your current levels and trends in key measures or indicators of workforce and leader development?
<--- Score

3. What alternative responses are available to manage risk?

<--- Score

4. How can skill-level changes improve EDR privileged access management?

<--- Score

5. How do you deal with EDR privileged access management risk?

<--- Score

6. What can you do to improve?

<--- Score

7. How do you mitigate EDR privileged access management risk?

<--- Score

8. How does your organization evaluate strategic EDR privileged access management success?

<--- Score

9. How do you manage EDR privileged access management risk?

<--- Score

10. How do you link measurement and risk?

<--- Score

11. What attendant changes will need to be made to ensure that the solution is successful?

<--- Score

12. Is a solution implementation plan established, including schedule/work breakdown structure,

resources, risk management plan, cost/budget, and control plan?

<--- Score

13. Does the goal represent a desired result that can be measured?

<--- Score

14. What are the affordable EDR privileged access management risks?

<--- Score

15. Where do the EDR privileged access management decisions reside?

<--- Score

16. Would you develop a EDR privileged access management Communication Strategy?

<--- Score

17. Is the EDR privileged access management solution sustainable?

<--- Score

18. How can you improve EDR privileged access management?

<--- Score

19. What went well, what should change, what can improve?

<--- Score

20. How is knowledge sharing about risk management improved?

<--- Score

21. What were the underlying assumptions on the cost-benefit analysis?
<--- Score

22. Explorations of the frontiers of EDR privileged access management will help you build influence, improve EDR privileged access management, optimize decision making, and sustain change, what is your approach?
<--- Score

23. What do you want to improve?
<--- Score

24. What are the concrete EDR privileged access management results?
<--- Score

25. How can the phases of EDR privileged access management development be identified?
<--- Score

26. What criteria will you use to assess your EDR privileged access management risks?
<--- Score

27. How do you decide how much to remunerate an employee?
<--- Score

28. How do you manage and improve your EDR privileged access management work systems to deliver customer value and achieve organizational success and sustainability?
<--- Score

29. How will you measure the results?
<--- Score

30. Was a pilot designed for the proposed solution(s)?
<--- Score

31. Do you have the optimal project management team structure?
<--- Score

32. What assumptions are made about the solution and approach?
<--- Score

33. Which of the recognised risks out of all risks can be most likely transferred?
<--- Score

34. What risks do you need to manage?
<--- Score

35. What does the 'should be' process map/design look like?
<--- Score

36. Are risk management tasks balanced centrally and locally?
<--- Score

37. How do you go about comparing EDR privileged access management approaches/solutions?
<--- Score

38. What area needs the greatest improvement?
<--- Score

39. What tools were used to evaluate the potential solutions?
<--- Score

40. What is the implementation plan?
<--- Score

41. Are the key business and technology risks being managed?
<--- Score

42. Is the optimal solution selected based on testing and analysis?
<--- Score

43. If you could go back in time five years, what decision would you make differently? What is your best guess as to what decision you're making today you might regret five years from now?
<--- Score

44. Is the solution technically practical?
<--- Score

45. Is the implementation plan designed?
<--- Score

46. Where do you need EDR privileged access management improvement?
<--- Score

47. How do you define the solutions' scope?
<--- Score

48. Is any EDR privileged access management documentation required?

<--- Score

49. What is EDR privileged access management's impact on utilizing the best solution(s)?
<--- Score

50. How can you improve performance?
<--- Score

51. How are EDR privileged access management risks managed?
<--- Score

52. Are the risks fully understood, reasonable and manageable?
<--- Score

53. What to do with the results or outcomes of measurements?
<--- Score

54. Risk Identification: What are the possible risk events your organization faces in relation to EDR privileged access management?
<--- Score

55. Do you need to do a usability evaluation?
<--- Score

56. How do the EDR privileged access management results compare with the performance of your competitors and other organizations with similar offerings?
<--- Score

57. Who do you report EDR privileged access

management results to?
<--- Score

58. Can you integrate quality management and risk management?
<--- Score

59. Who manages supplier risk management in your organization?
<--- Score

60. Is there a high likelihood that any recommendations will achieve their intended results?
<--- Score

61. How risky is your organization?
<--- Score

62. Was a EDR privileged access management charter developed?
<--- Score

63. Are the most efficient solutions problem-specific?
<--- Score

64. Is EDR privileged access management documentation maintained?
<--- Score

65. What is the team's contingency plan for potential problems occurring in implementation?
<--- Score

66. Is there a small-scale pilot for proposed improvement(s)? What conclusions were drawn from the outcomes of a pilot?

<--- Score

67. How are policy decisions made and where?
<--- Score

68. How is continuous improvement applied to risk management?
<--- Score

69. What should a proof of concept or pilot accomplish?
<--- Score

70. How will you know that you have improved?
<--- Score

71. What EDR privileged access management improvements can be made?
<--- Score

72. How will you know that a change is an improvement?
<--- Score

73. What communications are necessary to support the implementation of the solution?
<--- Score

74. Who controls the risk?
<--- Score

75. What tools do you use once you have decided on a EDR privileged access management strategy and more importantly how do you choose?
<--- Score

76. What needs improvement? Why?
<--- Score

77. Who should make the EDR privileged access management decisions?
<--- Score

78. What tools were used to tap into the creativity and encourage 'outside the box' thinking?
<--- Score

79. What practices helps your organization to develop its capacity to recognize patterns?
<--- Score

80. What tools were most useful during the improve phase?
<--- Score

81. Were any criteria developed to assist the team in testing and evaluating potential solutions?
<--- Score

82. How can you better manage risk?
<--- Score

83. For decision problems, how do you develop a decision statement?
<--- Score

84. What strategies for EDR privileged access management improvement are successful?
<--- Score

85. Who will be using the results of the measurement activities?

<--- Score

86. How do you measure risk?
<--- Score

87. Have you identified breakpoints and/or risk tolerances that will trigger broad consideration of a potential need for intervention or modification of strategy?
<--- Score

88. What is the magnitude of the improvements?
<--- Score

89. Is the EDR privileged access management risk managed?
<--- Score

90. Who manages EDR privileged access management risk?
<--- Score

91. Who are the people involved in developing and implementing EDR privileged access management?
<--- Score

92. Is there a cost/benefit analysis of optimal solution(s)?
<--- Score

93. Does a good decision guarantee a good outcome?
<--- Score

94. Who are the EDR privileged access management decision-makers?

<--- Score

95. Who are the EDR privileged access management decision makers?
<--- Score

96. To what extent does management recognize EDR privileged access management as a tool to increase the results?
<--- Score

97. Are you assessing EDR privileged access management and risk?
<--- Score

98. Is risk periodically assessed?
<--- Score

99. Is pilot data collected and analyzed?
<--- Score

100. What is the risk?
<--- Score

101. Is supporting EDR privileged access management documentation required?
<--- Score

102. Is the EDR privileged access management documentation thorough?
<--- Score

103. For estimation problems, how do you develop an estimation statement?
<--- Score

104. Is the scope clearly documented?

<--- Score

105. Do you cover the five essential competencies: Communication, Collaboration,Innovation, Adaptability, and Leadership that improve an organizations ability to leverage the new EDR privileged access management in a volatile global economy?

<--- Score

106. How do you improve your likelihood of success ?

<--- Score

107. How do you measure improved EDR privileged access management service perception, and satisfaction?

<--- Score

108. Are decisions made in a timely manner?

<--- Score

109. What improvements have been achieved?

<--- Score

110. Is there any other EDR privileged access management solution?

<--- Score

111. How will you know when its improved?

<--- Score

112. Are procedures documented for managing EDR privileged access management risks?

<--- Score

113. Can you identify any significant risks or exposures to EDR privileged access management third- parties (vendors, service providers, alliance partners etc) that concern you?
<--- Score

114. What were the criteria for evaluating a EDR privileged access management pilot?
<--- Score

115. Who do you report EDR privileged access management results to?
<--- Score

116. How will you recognize and celebrate results?
<--- Score

117. What current systems have to be understood and/or changed?
<--- Score

118. Are risk triggers captured?
<--- Score

119. Do vendor agreements bring new compliance risk ?
<--- Score

120. At what point will vulnerability assessments be performed once EDR privileged access management is put into production (e.g., ongoing Risk Management after implementation)?
<--- Score

121. How do you keep improving EDR privileged

access management?
<--- Score

122. In the past few months, what is the smallest change you have made that has had the biggest positive result? What was it about that small change that produced the large return?
<--- Score

123. What error proofing will be done to address some of the discrepancies observed in the 'as is' process?
<--- Score

124. How risky is your organization?
<--- Score

125. When you map the key players in your own work and the types/domains of relationships with them, which relationships do you find easy and which challenging, and why?
<--- Score

126. Is the measure of success for EDR privileged access management understandable to a variety of people?
<--- Score

127. What are the implications of the one critical EDR privileged access management decision 10 minutes, 10 months, and 10 years from now?
<--- Score

128. What lessons, if any, from a pilot were incorporated into the design of the full-scale solution?
<--- Score

129. Are events managed to resolution?
<--- Score

130. Who makes the EDR privileged access management decisions in your organization?
<--- Score

131. How do you improve productivity?
<--- Score

132. What actually has to improve and by how much?
<--- Score

133. Who controls key decisions that will be made?
<--- Score

134. Can the solution be designed and implemented within an acceptable time period?
<--- Score

135. EDR privileged access management risk decisions: whose call Is It?
<--- Score

136. Who will be responsible for making the decisions to include or exclude requested changes once EDR privileged access management is underway?
<--- Score

137. Who are the key stakeholders for the EDR privileged access management evaluation?
<--- Score

138. Have you achieved EDR privileged access management improvements?

<--- Score

139. How significant is the improvement in the eyes of the end user?
<--- Score

140. What is the EDR privileged access management's sustainability risk?
<--- Score

141. Who will be responsible for documenting the EDR privileged access management requirements in detail?
<--- Score

Add up total points for this section:
_ _ _ _ _ = Total points for this section

Divided by: _ _ _ _ _ _ (number of statements answered) = _ _ _ _ _ _
Average score for this section

Transfer your score to the EDR privileged access management Index at the beginning of the Self-Assessment.

CRITERION #6: CONTROL:

INTENT: Implement the practical solution. Maintain the performance and correct possible complications.

In my belief, the answer to this question is clearly defined:

5 Strongly Agree

4 Agree

3 Neutral

2 Disagree

1 Strongly Disagree

1. How will EDR privileged access management decisions be made and monitored?
<--- Score

2. Is knowledge gained on process shared and institutionalized?
<--- Score

3. Are there documented procedures?

<--- Score

4. How do you establish and deploy modified action plans if circumstances require a shift in plans and rapid execution of new plans?
<--- Score

5. What can you control?
<--- Score

6. How can you best use all of your knowledge repositories to enhance learning and sharing?
<--- Score

7. Who controls critical resources?
<--- Score

8. Does the response plan contain a definite closed loop continual improvement scheme (e.g., plan-do-check-act)?
<--- Score

9. What are customers monitoring?
<--- Score

10. Is a response plan established and deployed?
<--- Score

11. Has the improved process and its steps been standardized?
<--- Score

12. What are the critical parameters to watch?
<--- Score

13. Will your goals reflect your program budget?

<--- Score

14. How do you select, collect, align, and integrate EDR privileged access management data and information for tracking daily operations and overall organizational performance, including progress relative to strategic objectives and action plans?
<--- Score

15. How do you plan on providing proper recognition and disclosure of supporting companies?
<--- Score

16. Does job training on the documented procedures need to be part of the process team's education and training?
<--- Score

17. How likely is the current EDR privileged access management plan to come in on schedule or on budget?
<--- Score

18. Is there a transfer of ownership and knowledge to process owner and process team tasked with the responsibilities.
<--- Score

19. How do you encourage people to take control and responsibility?
<--- Score

20. What should you measure to verify efficiency gains?

<--- Score

21. Will existing staff require re-training, for example, to learn new business processes?
<--- Score

22. Is there an action plan in case of emergencies?
<--- Score

23. Are new process steps, standards, and documentation ingrained into normal operations?
<--- Score

24. What is the recommended frequency of auditing?
<--- Score

25. What are your results for key measures or indicators of the accomplishment of your EDR privileged access management strategy and action plans, including building and strengthening core competencies?
<--- Score

26. Do you monitor the effectiveness of your EDR privileged access management activities?
<--- Score

27. Do you monitor the EDR privileged access management decisions made and fine tune them as they evolve?
<--- Score

28. What should the next improvement project be that is related to EDR privileged access management?
<--- Score

29. Who will be in control?
<--- Score

30. Are the EDR privileged access management standards challenging?
<--- Score

31. Are operating procedures consistent?
<--- Score

32. Can you adapt and adjust to changing EDR privileged access management situations?
<--- Score

33. What is the best design framework for EDR privileged access management organization now that, in a post industrial-age if the top-down, command and control model is no longer relevant?
<--- Score

34. How do senior leaders actions reflect a commitment to the organizations EDR privileged access management values?
<--- Score

35. Are controls in place and consistently applied?
<--- Score

36. Do the EDR privileged access management decisions you make today help people and the planet tomorrow?
<--- Score

37. Does the EDR privileged access management performance meet the customer's requirements?
<--- Score

38. What is the control/monitoring plan?
<--- Score

39. How do you spread information?
<--- Score

40. Is there a standardized process?
<--- Score

41. How do you monitor usage and cost?
<--- Score

42. What do your reports reflect?
<--- Score

43. Does a troubleshooting guide exist or is it needed?
<--- Score

44. How do you plan for the cost of succession?
<--- Score

45. Is there a recommended audit plan for routine surveillance inspections of EDR privileged access management's gains?
<--- Score

46. What EDR privileged access management standards are applicable?
<--- Score

47. Is the EDR privileged access management test/ monitoring cost justified?
<--- Score

48. Have new or revised work instructions resulted?

<--- Score

49. Is new knowledge gained imbedded in the response plan?
<--- Score

50. How will new or emerging customer needs/requirements be checked/communicated to orient the process toward meeting the new specifications and continually reducing variation?
<--- Score

51. Are the planned controls in place?
<--- Score

52. Act/Adjust: What Do you Need to Do Differently?
<--- Score

53. What are the performance and scale of the EDR privileged access management tools?
<--- Score

54. What are the key elements of your EDR privileged access management performance improvement system, including your evaluation, organizational learning, and innovation processes?
<--- Score

55. Is there a documented and implemented monitoring plan?
<--- Score

56. Are you measuring, monitoring and predicting EDR privileged access management activities to

optimize operations and profitability, and enhancing outcomes?
<--- Score

57. How might the group capture best practices and lessons learned so as to leverage improvements?
<--- Score

58. What do you stand for--and what are you against?
<--- Score

59. How widespread is its use?
<--- Score

60. What are the known security controls?
<--- Score

61. Who is going to spread your message?
<--- Score

62. Has the EDR privileged access management value of standards been quantified?
<--- Score

63. What is your plan to assess your security risks?
<--- Score

64. Are suggested corrective/restorative actions indicated on the response plan for known causes to problems that might surface?
<--- Score

65. Can support from partners be adjusted?
<--- Score

66. Is a response plan in place for when the input,

process, or output measures indicate an 'out-of-control' condition?

<--- Score

67. Is there a EDR privileged access management Communication plan covering who needs to get what information when?

<--- Score

68. How will input, process, and output variables be checked to detect for sub-optimal conditions?

<--- Score

69. Is reporting being used or needed?

<--- Score

70. Who sets the EDR privileged access management standards?

<--- Score

71. What is your theory of human motivation, and how does your compensation plan fit with that view?

<--- Score

72. What other systems, operations, processes, and infrastructures (hiring practices, staffing, training, incentives/rewards, metrics/dashboards/scorecards, etc.) need updates, additions, changes, or deletions in order to facilitate knowledge transfer and improvements?

<--- Score

73. Where do ideas that reach policy makers and planners as proposals for EDR privileged access management strengthening and reform actually

originate?
<--- Score

74. Are documented procedures clear and easy to follow for the operators?
<--- Score

75. How do your controls stack up?
<--- Score

76. Who is the EDR privileged access management process owner?
<--- Score

77. How will the process owner verify improvement in present and future sigma levels, process capabilities?
<--- Score

78. Is there a control plan in place for sustaining improvements (short and long-term)?
<--- Score

79. How will the process owner and team be able to hold the gains?
<--- Score

80. Will the team be available to assist members in planning investigations?
<--- Score

81. In the case of a EDR privileged access management project, the criteria for the audit derive from implementation objectives, an audit of a EDR privileged access management project involves assessing whether the recommendations outlined for implementation have been met, can you track that

any EDR privileged access management project is implemented as planned, and is it working?
<--- Score

82. How will report readings be checked to effectively monitor performance?
<--- Score

83. Does EDR privileged access management appropriately measure and monitor risk?
<--- Score

84. How is change control managed?
<--- Score

85. How will the day-to-day responsibilities for monitoring and continual improvement be transferred from the improvement team to the process owner?
<--- Score

86. What are you attempting to measure/monitor?
<--- Score

87. Are the planned controls working?
<--- Score

88. What other areas of the group might benefit from the EDR privileged access management team's improvements, knowledge, and learning?
<--- Score

89. What is the standard for acceptable EDR privileged access management performance?
<--- Score

90. What quality tools were useful in the control phase?
<--- Score

91. What adjustments to the strategies are needed?
<--- Score

92. What do you measure to verify effectiveness gains?
<--- Score

93. Against what alternative is success being measured?
<--- Score

94. Will any special training be provided for results interpretation?
<--- Score

95. Implementation Planning: is a pilot needed to test the changes before a full roll out occurs?
<--- Score

96. What key inputs and outputs are being measured on an ongoing basis?
<--- Score

97. Do the viable solutions scale to future needs?
<--- Score

98. Is there documentation that will support the successful operation of the improvement?
<--- Score

Add up total points for this section:
_ _ _ _ _ = Total points for this section

Divided by: _____ (number of
statements answered) = _____
Average score for this section

Transfer your score to the EDR
privileged access management Index at
the beginning of the Self-Assessment.

CRITERION #7: SUSTAIN:

INTENT: Retain the benefits.

In my belief, the answer to this question is clearly defined:

5 Strongly Agree

4 Agree

3 Neutral

2 Disagree

1 Strongly Disagree

1. If you had to rebuild your organization without any traditional competitive advantages (i.e., no killer technology, promising research, innovative product/service delivery model, etcetera), how would your people have to approach their work and collaborate together in order to create the necessary conditions for success?
<--- Score

2. Is maximizing EDR privileged access management protection the same as minimizing EDR privileged

access management loss?
<--- Score

3. Which individuals, teams or departments will be involved in EDR privileged access management?
<--- Score

4. What goals did you miss?
<--- Score

5. How do you lead with EDR privileged access management in mind?
<--- Score

6. How likely is it that a customer would recommend your company to a friend or colleague?
<--- Score

7. Are all key stakeholders present at all Structured Walkthroughs?
<--- Score

8. How do you determine the key elements that affect EDR privileged access management workforce satisfaction, how are these elements determined for different workforce groups and segments?
<--- Score

9. What are the gaps in your knowledge and experience?
<--- Score

10. Are you making progress, and are you making progress as EDR privileged access management

leaders?
<--- Score

11. What happens at your organization when people fail?
<--- Score

12. What are the success criteria that will indicate that EDR privileged access management objectives have been met and the benefits delivered?
<--- Score

13. How do you accomplish your long range EDR privileged access management goals?
<--- Score

14. Can you do all this work?
<--- Score

15. Operational - will it work?
<--- Score

16. Would you rather sell to knowledgeable and informed customers or to uninformed customers?
<--- Score

17. What business benefits will EDR privileged access management goals deliver if achieved?
<--- Score

18. What would have to be true for the option on the table to be the best possible choice?
<--- Score

19. Marketing budgets are tighter, consumers are more skeptical, and social media has changed

forever the way we talk about EDR privileged access management, how do you gain traction?
<--- Score

20. What are the potential basics of EDR privileged access management fraud?
<--- Score

21. Who are four people whose careers you have enhanced?
<--- Score

22. If you find that you havent accomplished one of the goals for one of the steps of the EDR privileged access management strategy, what will you do to fix it?
<--- Score

23. Is a EDR privileged access management team work effort in place?
<--- Score

24. What EDR privileged access management modifications can you make work for you?
<--- Score

25. What have you done to protect your business from competitive encroachment?
<--- Score

26. Which functions and people interact with the supplier and or customer?
<--- Score

27. What counts that you are not counting?
<--- Score

28. If you were responsible for initiating and implementing major changes in your organization, what steps might you take to ensure acceptance of those changes?
<--- Score

29. What information is critical to your organization that your executives are ignoring?
<--- Score

30. How do you transition from the baseline to the target?
<--- Score

31. What is your question? Why?
<--- Score

32. What is the estimated value of the project?
<--- Score

33. What one word do you want to own in the minds of your customers, employees, and partners?
<--- Score

34. Is it economical; do you have the time and money?
<--- Score

35. What happens when a new employee joins the organization?
<--- Score

36. What does your signature ensure?
<--- Score

37. Why will customers want to buy your

organizations products/services?

<--- Score

38. What are strategies for increasing support and reducing opposition?

<--- Score

39. Why do and why don't your customers like your organization?

<--- Score

40. Who are the key stakeholders?

<--- Score

41. What is your EDR privileged access management strategy?

<--- Score

42. Are you / should you be revolutionary or evolutionary?

<--- Score

43. How do you manage EDR privileged access management Knowledge Management (KM)?

<--- Score

44. Which models, tools and techniques are necessary?

<--- Score

45. What is something you believe that nearly no one agrees with you on?

<--- Score

46. Are the criteria for selecting recommendations stated?

<--- Score

47. Is your basic point _____ or _____?
<--- Score

48. What is the overall business strategy?
<--- Score

49. What is the source of the strategies for EDR privileged access management strengthening and reform?
<--- Score

50. Are assumptions made in EDR privileged access management stated explicitly?
<--- Score

51. Is a EDR privileged access management breakthrough on the horizon?
<--- Score

52. Why is it important to have senior management support for a EDR privileged access management project?
<--- Score

53. What is the recommended frequency of auditing?
<--- Score

54. Is there a work around that you can use?
<--- Score

55. When information truly is ubiquitous, when reach and connectivity are completely global, when computing resources are infinite, and when a whole new set of impossibilities are not only possible, but

happening, what will that do to your business?
<--- Score

56. What are the rules and assumptions your industry operates under? What if the opposite were true?
<--- Score

57. How do senior leaders deploy your organizations vision and values through your leadership system, to the workforce, to key suppliers and partners, and to customers and other stakeholders, as appropriate?
<--- Score

58. Instead of going to current contacts for new ideas, what if you reconnected with dormant contacts-- the people you used to know? If you were going reactivate a dormant tie, who would it be?
<--- Score

59. What new services of functionality will be implemented next with EDR privileged access management ?
<--- Score

60. Who else should you help?
<--- Score

61. How are you doing compared to your industry?
<--- Score

62. What did you miss in the interview for the worst hire you ever made?
<--- Score

63. Can you maintain your growth without

detracting from the factors that have contributed to your success?
<--- Score

64. Will there be any necessary staff changes (redundancies or new hires)?
<--- Score

65. How do you foster the skills, knowledge, talents, attributes, and characteristics you want to have?
<--- Score

66. What could happen if you do not do it?
<--- Score

67. What are the barriers to increased EDR privileged access management production?
<--- Score

68. What EDR privileged access management skills are most important?
<--- Score

69. Who are your customers?
<--- Score

70. What is your formula for success in EDR privileged access management ?
<--- Score

71. What is the funding source for this project?
<--- Score

72. Who, on the executive team or the board, has spoken to a customer recently?
<--- Score

73. How can you incorporate support to ensure safe and effective use of EDR privileged access management into the services that you provide?
<--- Score

74. Who is responsible for errors?
<--- Score

75. Why not do EDR privileged access management?
<--- Score

76. Who will be responsible for deciding whether EDR privileged access management goes ahead or not after the initial investigations?
<--- Score

77. What have been your experiences in defining long range EDR privileged access management goals?
<--- Score

78. What stupid rule would you most like to kill?
<--- Score

79. Is the EDR privileged access management organization completing tasks effectively and efficiently?
<--- Score

80. How important is EDR privileged access management to the user organizations mission?
<--- Score

81. Do you think you know, or do you know you know ?

<--- Score

82. What are the business goals EDR privileged access management is aiming to achieve?
<--- Score

83. Are you satisfied with your current role? If not, what is missing from it?
<--- Score

84. What is the craziest thing you can do?
<--- Score

85. Is EDR privileged access management dependent on the successful delivery of a current project?
<--- Score

86. What are you challenging?
<--- Score

87. Do you know what you are doing? And who do you call if you don't?
<--- Score

88. Are there any activities that you can take off your to do list?
<--- Score

89. Is your strategy driving your strategy? Or is the way in which you allocate resources driving your strategy?
<--- Score

90. Do you feel that more should be done in the EDR privileged access management area?
<--- Score

91. What may be the consequences for the performance of an organization if all stakeholders are not consulted regarding EDR privileged access management?

<--- Score

92. How do you stay inspired?

<--- Score

93. Who do you think the world wants your organization to be?

<--- Score

94. Is there any reason to believe the opposite of my current belief?

<--- Score

95. What is the overall talent health of your organization as a whole at senior levels, and for each organization reporting to a member of the Senior Leadership Team?

<--- Score

96. How do you foster innovation?

<--- Score

97. Political -is anyone trying to undermine this project?

<--- Score

98. What trophy do you want on your mantle?

<--- Score

99. What projects are going on in the organization today, and what resources are those projects using

from the resource pools?
<--- Score

100. Is there any existing EDR privileged access management governance structure?
<--- Score

101. How will you insure seamless interoperability of EDR privileged access management moving forward?
<--- Score

102. What you are going to do to affect the numbers?
<--- Score

103. Who is responsible for EDR privileged access management?
<--- Score

104. Has implementation been effective in reaching specified objectives so far?
<--- Score

105. What are the short and long-term EDR privileged access management goals?
<--- Score

106. What was the last experiment you ran?
<--- Score

107. What are the key enablers to make this EDR privileged access management move?
<--- Score

108. If no one would ever find out about your accomplishments, how would you lead differently?
<--- Score

109. What is a feasible sequencing of reform initiatives over time?
<--- Score

110. Do you have enough freaky customers in your portfolio pushing you to the limit day in and day out?
<--- Score

111. In a project to restructure EDR privileged access management outcomes, which stakeholders would you involve?
<--- Score

112. Who is responsible for ensuring appropriate resources (time, people and money) are allocated to EDR privileged access management?
<--- Score

113. How do you proactively clarify deliverables and EDR privileged access management quality expectations?
<--- Score

114. Who will provide the final approval of EDR privileged access management deliverables?
<--- Score

115. How is implementation research currently incorporated into each of your goals?
<--- Score

116. How do you maintain EDR privileged access management's Integrity?
<--- Score

117. Whom among your colleagues do you trust, and for what?
<--- Score

118. How do you provide a safe environment -physically and emotionally?
<--- Score

119. Who do we want your customers to become?
<--- Score

120. What is the purpose of EDR privileged access management in relation to the mission?
<--- Score

121. How will you know that the EDR privileged access management project has been successful?
<--- Score

122. In retrospect, of the projects that you pulled the plug on, what percent do you wish had been allowed to keep going, and what percent do you wish had ended earlier?
<--- Score

123. Will it be accepted by users?
<--- Score

124. How will you ensure you get what you expected?
<--- Score

125. How do you keep the momentum going?
<--- Score

126. How do you govern and fulfill your societal

responsibilities?
<--- Score

127. What are current EDR privileged access management paradigms?
<--- Score

128. What will be the consequences to the stakeholder (financial, reputation etc) if EDR privileged access management does not go ahead or fails to deliver the objectives?
<--- Score

129. What is the big EDR privileged access management idea?
<--- Score

130. What are the challenges?
<--- Score

131. Do you have past EDR privileged access management successes?
<--- Score

132. At what moment would you think; Will I get fired?
<--- Score

133. How do you engage the workforce, in addition to satisfying them?
<--- Score

134. What relationships among EDR privileged access management trends do you perceive?
<--- Score

135. How do you go about securing EDR privileged access management?
<--- Score

136. Do you have the right capabilities and capacities?
<--- Score

137. Who do you want your customers to become?
<--- Score

138. What are internal and external EDR privileged access management relations?
<--- Score

139. What is the range of capabilities?
<--- Score

140. Ask yourself: how would you do this work if you only had one staff member to do it?
<--- Score

141. How do you make it meaningful in connecting EDR privileged access management with what users do day-to-day?
<--- Score

142. What are your personal philosophies regarding EDR privileged access management and how do they influence your work?
<--- Score

143. Can the schedule be done in the given time?
<--- Score

144. What potential megatrends could make your business model obsolete?

<--- Score

145. Who is on the team?
<--- Score

146. How do you keep records, of what?
<--- Score

147. How do customers see your organization?
<--- Score

148. What is the kind of project structure that would be appropriate for your EDR privileged access management project, should it be formal and complex, or can it be less formal and relatively simple?
<--- Score

149. What is an unauthorized commitment?
<--- Score

150. Why is EDR privileged access management important for you now?
<--- Score

151. What knowledge, skills and characteristics mark a good EDR privileged access management project manager?
<--- Score

152. What is your BATNA (best alternative to a negotiated agreement)?
<--- Score

153. To whom do you add value?
<--- Score

154. Who is the main stakeholder, with ultimate responsibility for driving EDR privileged access management forward?
<--- Score

155. Are the assumptions believable and achievable?
<--- Score

156. Do you think EDR privileged access management accomplishes the goals you expect it to accomplish?
<--- Score

157. How do you set EDR privileged access management stretch targets and how do you get people to not only participate in setting these stretch targets but also that they strive to achieve these?
<--- Score

158. What trouble can you get into?
<--- Score

159. Who have you, as a company, historically been when you've been at your best?
<--- Score

160. How do you deal with EDR privileged access management changes?
<--- Score

161. Are you maintaining a past–present–future perspective throughout the EDR privileged access management discussion?
<--- Score

162. What would you recommend your friend do if he/she were facing this dilemma?

<--- Score

163. Is EDR privileged access management realistic, or are you setting yourself up for failure?
<--- Score

164. How do you track customer value, profitability or financial return, organizational success, and sustainability?
<--- Score

165. Think of your EDR privileged access management project, what are the main functions?
<--- Score

166. What are the top 3 things at the forefront of your EDR privileged access management agendas for the next 3 years?
<--- Score

167. Did your employees make progress today?
<--- Score

168. Why should people listen to you?
<--- Score

169. How long will it take to change?
<--- Score

170. Which EDR privileged access management goals are the most important?
<--- Score

171. What role does communication play in the success or failure of a EDR privileged access management project?

<--- Score

172. Whose voice (department, ethnic group, women, older workers, etc) might you have missed hearing from in your company, and how might you amplify this voice to create positive momentum for your business?
<--- Score

173. What are the long-term EDR privileged access management goals?
<--- Score

174. Who uses your product in ways you never expected?
<--- Score

175. What unique value proposition (UVP) do you offer?
<--- Score

176. If you do not follow, then how to lead?
<--- Score

Add up total points for this section:
_ _ _ _ _ = Total points for this section

Divided by: _ _ _ _ _ _ (number of statements answered) = _ _ _ _ _ _
Average score for this section

Transfer your score to the EDR privileged access management Index at the beginning of the Self-Assessment.

EDR Privileged Access Management and Managing Projects, Criteria for Project Managers:

1.0 Initiating Process Group: EDR Privileged Access Management

1. Did you use a contractor or vendor?

2. If action is called for, what form should it take?

3. Who does what?

4. Do you know the EDR Privileged Access Management projects goal, purpose and objectives?

5. How well did you do?

6. What were things that you did very well and want to do the same again on the next EDR Privileged Access Management project?

7. What areas does the group agree are the biggest success on the EDR Privileged Access Management project?

8. Have the stakeholders identified all individual requirements pertaining to business process?

9. The EDR Privileged Access Management project managers have maximum authority in which type of organization?

10. Did the EDR Privileged Access Management project team have the right skills?

11. What must be done?

12. How well did the chosen processes produce the

expected results?

13. Which six sigma dmaic phase focuses on why and how defects and errors occur?

14. What are the inputs required to produce the deliverables?

15. Who supports, improves, and oversees standardized processes related to the EDR Privileged Access Management projects program?

16. First of all, should any action be taken?

17. How will it affect me?

18. What are the short and long term implications?

19. Are you properly tracking the progress of the EDR Privileged Access Management project and communicating the status to stakeholders?

20. What were the challenges that you encountered during the execution of a previous EDR Privileged Access Management project that you would not want to repeat?

1.1 Project Charter: EDR Privileged Access Management

21. Pop quiz – which are the same inputs as in the EDR Privileged Access Management project charter?

22. Who are the stakeholders?

23. Assumptions: what factors, for planning purposes, are you considering to be true?

24. Why Outsource?

25. What are the assigned resources?

26. Major high-level milestone targets: what events measure progress?

27. What metrics could you look at?

28. Are you building in-house ?

29. EDR Privileged Access Management project objective statement: what must the EDR Privileged Access Management project do?

30. Strategic fit: what is the strategic initiative identifier for this EDR Privileged Access Management project?

31. When?

32. Who is the sponsor?

33. Why is a EDR Privileged Access Management project Charter used?

34. What does it need to do?

35. Customer benefits: what customer requirements does this EDR Privileged Access Management project address?

36. Why do you manage integration?

37. For whom?

38. Why have you chosen the aim you have set forth?

39. How much?

40. Where does all this information come from?

1.2 Stakeholder Register: EDR Privileged Access Management

41. What & Why?

42. What are the major EDR Privileged Access Management project milestones requiring communications or providing communications opportunities?

43. Is your organization ready for change?

44. Who is managing stakeholder engagement?

45. How should employers make voices heard?

46. How big is the gap?

47. What opportunities exist to provide communications?

48. How will reports be created?

49. What is the power of the stakeholder?

50. Who wants to talk about Security?

51. How much influence do they have on the EDR Privileged Access Management project?

1.3 Stakeholder Analysis Matrix: EDR Privileged Access Management

52. Processes and systems, etc?

53. What advantages do your organizations stakeholders have?

54. Lack of competitive strength?

55. Seasonality, weather effects?

56. Which conditions out of the control of the management are crucial for the sustainability of its effects?

57. Business and product development?

58. If the baseline is now, and if its improved it will be better than now?

59. Who will promote/support the EDR Privileged Access Management project, provided that they are involved?

60. How to measure the achievement of the Outputs?

61. Advantages of proposition?

62. Will the impacts be local, national or international?

63. What is in it for you?

64. What unique or lowest-cost resources does the EDR Privileged Access Management project have access to?

65. Innovative aspects?

66. How do you manage EDR Privileged Access Management project Risk?

67. How will the stakeholder directly benefit from the EDR Privileged Access Management project and how will this affect the stakeholders motivation?

68. Partnership opportunities/synergies?

69. Who has the power to influence the outcomes of the work?

70. Who are potential allies and opponents?

71. Global influences?

2.0 Planning Process Group: EDR Privileged Access Management

72. What makes your EDR Privileged Access Management project successful?

73. What is involved in EDR Privileged Access Management project scope management, and why is good EDR Privileged Access Management project scope management so important on information technology EDR Privileged Access Management projects?

74. How does activity resource estimation affect activity duration estimation?

75. What factors are contributing to progress or delay in the achievement of products and results?

76. What is the NEXT thing to do?

77. Contingency planning. if a risk event occurs, what will you do?

78. To what extent do the intervention objectives and strategies of the EDR Privileged Access Management project respond to your organizations plans?

79. If you are late, will anybody notice?

80. To what extent has the intervention strategy been adapted to the areas of intervention in which it is being implemented?

81. What good practices or successful experiences or transferable examples have been identified?

82. When developing the estimates for EDR Privileged Access Management project phases, you choose to add the individual estimates for the activities that comprise each phase. What type of estimation method are you using?

83. Why do it EDR Privileged Access Management projects fail?

84. If a risk event occurs, what will you do?

85. To what extent have public/private national resources and/or counterparts been mobilized to contribute to the programs objective and produce results and impacts?

86. What business situation is being addressed?

87. Do the partners have sufficient financial capacity to keep up the benefits produced by the programme?

88. In what way has the program contributed towards the issue culture and development included on the public agenda?

89. What should you do next?

90. You did your readings, yes?

91. Does it make any difference if you are successful?

2.1 Project Management Plan: EDR Privileged Access Management

92. Has the selected plan been formulated using cost effectiveness and incremental analysis techniques?

93. Is there an incremental analysis/cost effectiveness analysis of proposed mitigation features based on an approved method and using an accepted model?

94. How do you manage time?

95. What would you do differently?

96. Did the planning effort collaborate to develop solutions that integrate expertise, policies, programs, and EDR Privileged Access Management projects across entities?

97. Is the budget realistic?

98. What is the justification?

99. What should you drop in order to add something new?

100. If the EDR Privileged Access Management project management plan is a comprehensive document that guides you in EDR Privileged Access Management project execution and control, then what should it NOT contain?

101. When is the EDR Privileged Access Management

project management plan created?

102. Was the peer (technical) review of the cost estimates duly coordinated with the cost estimate center of expertise and addressed in the review documentation and certification?

103. What are the known stakeholder requirements?

104. Why Change?

105. What data/reports/tools/etc. do program managers need?

106. Do the proposed changes from the EDR Privileged Access Management project include any significant risks to safety?

107. Are there any client staffing expectations?

108. What if, for example, the positive direction and vision of your organization causes expected trends to change resulting in greater need than expected?

109. How well are you able to manage your risk?

2.2 Scope Management Plan: EDR Privileged Access Management

110. Do EDR Privileged Access Management project teams & team members report on status / activities / progress?

111. What went right?

112. Are measurements and feedback mechanisms incorporated in tracking work effort & refining work estimating techniques?

113. Are you doing what you have set out to do?

114. Are schedule deliverables actually delivered?

115. Describe how the deliverables will be verified against the EDR Privileged Access Management project scope. To whom will the deliverables be first presented for inspection and verification?

116. What went wrong?

117. What problem is being solved by delivering this EDR Privileged Access Management project?

118. Do you have the reasons why the changes to your organizational systems and capabilities are required?

119. Are risk triggers captured?

120. Are meeting objectives identified for each meeting?

121. Do you have funding for EDR Privileged Access Management project and product development, implementation and on-going support?

122. Why do you need to manage scope?

123. Is there an onboarding process in place?

124. Does the detailed work plan match the complexity of tasks with the capabilities of personnel?

125. Are estimating assumptions and constraints captured?

126. Has the EDR Privileged Access Management project approach and development strategy of the EDR Privileged Access Management project been defined, documented and accepted by the appropriate stakeholders?

127. Are post milestone EDR Privileged Access Management project reviews (PMPR) conducted with your organization at least once a year?

128. Have all unresolved risks been documented?

129. Are alternatives safe, functional, constructible, economical, reasonable and sustainable?

2.3 Requirements Management Plan: EDR Privileged Access Management

130. After the requirements are gathered and set forth on the requirements register, theyre little more than a laundry list of items. Some may be duplicates, some might conflict with others and some will be too broad or too vague to understand. Describe how the requirements will be analyzed. Who will perform the analysis?

131. Do you understand the role that each stakeholder will play in the requirements process?

132. Is there formal agreement on who has authority to approve a change in requirements?

133. How will the requirements become prioritized?

134. How will bidders price evaluations be done, by deliverables, phases, or in a big bang?

135. Is stakeholder risk tolerance an important factor for the requirements process in this EDR Privileged Access Management project?

136. Business analysis scope?

137. Is any organizational data being used or stored?

138. What performance metrics will be used?

139. Are actual resources expenditures versus planned

expenditures acceptable?

140. Is the change control process documented?

141. Do you really need to write this document at all?

142. Is requirements work dependent on any other specific EDR Privileged Access Management project or non-EDR Privileged Access Management project activities (e.g. funding, approvals, procurement)?

143. Have stakeholders been instructed in the Change Control process?

144. Controlling EDR Privileged Access Management project requirements involves monitoring the status of the EDR Privileged Access Management project requirements and managing changes to the requirements. Who is responsible for monitoring and tracking the EDR Privileged Access Management project requirements?

145. Will you perform a Requirements Risk assessment and develop a plan to deal with risks?

146. What information regarding the EDR Privileged Access Management project requirements will be reported?

147. Does the EDR Privileged Access Management project have a Change Control process?

148. Did you use declarative statements?

149. Who will approve the requirements (and if multiple approvers, in what order)?

2.4 Requirements Documentation: EDR Privileged Access Management

150. What is the risk associated with the technology?

151. Is the requirement properly understood?

152. Are all functions required by the customer included?

153. Is the origin of the requirement clearly stated?

154. Who provides requirements?

155. Where are business rules being captured?

156. Who is interacting with the system?

157. How will requirements be documented and who signs off on them?

158. Validity. does the system provide the functions which best support the customers needs?

159. Where do system and software requirements come from, what are sources?

160. How do you get the user to tell you what they want?

161. What marketing channels do you want to use: e-mail, letter or sms?

162. Does your organization restrict technical alternatives?

163. Are there any requirements conflicts?

164. Basic work/business process; high-level, what is being touched?

165. Do your constraints stand?

166. How will the proposed EDR Privileged Access Management project help?

167. What if the system wasn t implemented?

168. Consistency. are there any requirements conflicts?

169. Are there legal issues?

2.5 Requirements Traceability Matrix: EDR Privileged Access Management

170. How do you manage scope?

171. Is there a requirements traceability process in place?

172. How small is small enough?

173. What percentage of EDR Privileged Access Management projects are producing traceability matrices between requirements and other work products?

174. How will it affect the stakeholders personally in career?

175. Why use a WBS?

176. Do you have a clear understanding of all subcontracts in place?

177. Describe the process for approving requirements so they can be added to the traceability matrix and EDR Privileged Access Management project work can be performed. Will the EDR Privileged Access Management project requirements become approved in writing?

178. Will you use a Requirements Traceability Matrix?

179. Why do you manage scope?

180. What are the chronologies, contingencies, consequences, criteria?

181. What is the WBS?

2.6 Project Scope Statement: EDR Privileged Access Management

182. What is a process you might recommend to verify the accuracy of the research deliverable?

183. Did your EDR Privileged Access Management project ask for this?

184. How will you verify the accuracy of the work of the EDR Privileged Access Management project, and what constitutes acceptance of the deliverables?

185. Will the qa related information be reported regularly as part of the status reporting mechanisms?

186. Is the EDR Privileged Access Management project organization documented and on file?

187. Do you anticipate new stakeholders joining the EDR Privileged Access Management project over time?

188. Will statistics related to QA be collected, trends analyzed, and problems raised as issues?

189. What are the possible consequences should a risk come to occur?

190. What is the most common tool for helping define the detail?

191. What are the defined meeting materials?

192. Which risks does the EDR Privileged Access Management project focus on?

193. Will the risk plan be updated on a regular and frequent basis?

194. Will all EDR Privileged Access Management project issues be unconditionally tracked through the issue resolution process?

195. Any new risks introduced or old risks impacted. Are there issues that could affect the existing requirements for the result, service, or product if the scope changes?

196. Will the EDR Privileged Access Management project risks be managed according to the EDR Privileged Access Management projects risk management process?

197. Are there adequate EDR Privileged Access Management project control systems?

198. Will the risk documents be filed?

199. If there is an independent oversight contractor, have they signed off on the EDR Privileged Access Management project Plan?

200. If there are vendors, have they signed off on the EDR Privileged Access Management project Plan?

201. Where and how does the team fit within your organization structure?

2.7 Assumption and Constraint Log: EDR Privileged Access Management

202. Would known impacts serve as impediments?

203. How can you prevent/fix violations?

204. Violation trace: why ?

205. How do you design an auditing system?

206. Are there unnecessary steps that are creating bottlenecks and/or causing people to wait?

207. Do documented requirements exist for all critical components and areas, including technical, business, interfaces, performance, security and conversion requirements?

208. Have you eliminated all duplicative tasks or manual efforts, where appropriate?

209. When can log be discarded?

210. Are there nonconformance issues?

211. Is the definition of the EDR Privileged Access Management project scope clear; what needs to be accomplished?

212. Have all involved stakeholders and work groups committed to the EDR Privileged Access Management project?

213. How many EDR Privileged Access Management project staff does this specific process affect?

214. Model-building: what data-analytic strategies are useful when building proportional-hazards models?

215. Have adequate resources been provided by management to ensure EDR Privileged Access Management project success?

216. Are best practices and metrics employed to identify issues, progress, performance, etc.?

217. Is there a Steering Committee in place?

218. Does a specific action and/or state that is known to violate security policy occur?

219. Are there cosmetic errors that hinder readability and comprehension?

220. What worked well?

2.8 Work Breakdown Structure: EDR Privileged Access Management

221. Is it a change in scope?

222. What has to be done?

223. How will you and your EDR Privileged Access Management project team define the EDR Privileged Access Management projects scope and work breakdown structure?

224. Who has to do it?

225. When would you develop a Work Breakdown Structure?

226. Do you need another level?

227. What is the probability of completing the EDR Privileged Access Management project in less that xx days?

228. Is the work breakdown structure (wbs) defined and is the scope of the EDR Privileged Access Management project clear with assigned deliverable owners?

229. Is it still viable?

230. Can you make it?

231. When does it have to be done?

232. How much detail?

233. How far down?

234. What is the probability that the EDR Privileged Access Management project duration will exceed xx weeks?

235. Why would you develop a Work Breakdown Structure?

236. How many levels?

237. How big is a work-package?

238. When do you stop?

239. Where does it take place?

2.9 WBS Dictionary: EDR Privileged Access Management

240. Are estimates of costs at completion generated in a rational, consistent manner?

241. Is undistributed budget limited to contract effort which cannot yet be planned to CWBS elements at or below the level specified for reporting to the Government?

242. Are EDR Privileged Access Management projected overhead costs in each pool and the associated direct costs used as the basis for establishing interim rates for allocating overhead to contracts?

243. What are you counting on?

244. Can the contractor substantiate work package and planning package budgets?

245. Identify potential or actual budget-based and time-based schedule variances?

246. Does the contractors system description or procedures require that the performance measurement baseline plus management reserve equal the contract budget base?

247. Is future work which cannot be planned in detail subdivided to the extent practicable for budgeting and scheduling purposes?

248. Are work packages assigned to performing organizations?

249. Are the responsibilities and authorities of each of the above organizational elements or managers clearly defined?

250. Are overhead cost budgets established for each organization which has authority to incur overhead costs?

251. Are overhead costs budgets established on a basis consistent with anticipated direct business base?

252. Intermediate schedules, as required, which provide a logical sequence from the master schedule to the control account level?

253. Where engineering standards or other internal work measurement systems are used, is there a formal relationship between corresponding values and work package budgets?

254. Are time-phased budgets established for planning and control of level of effort activity by category of resource; for example, type of manpower and/or material?

255. Are the requirements for all items of overhead established by rational, traceable processes?

256. Are management actions taken to reduce indirect costs when there are significant adverse variances?

257. Are the bases and rates for allocating costs from
. each indirect pool consistently applied?

258. Are material costs reported within the same
period as that in which BCWP is earned for that
material?

2.10 Schedule Management Plan: EDR Privileged Access Management

259. What weaknesses do you have?

260. Is pert / critical path or equivalent methodology being used?

261. Will the tools selected accomplish the scheduling needs?

262. Does the schedule have reasonable float?

263. What tools and techniques will be used to estimate activity durations?

264. Are changes in deliverable commitments agreed to by all affected groups & individuals?

265. Is the schedule vertically and horizontally traceable?

266. Are the quality tools and methods identified in the Quality Plan appropriate to the EDR Privileged Access Management project?

267. Is a process defined for baseline approval and control?

268. Are multiple estimation methods being employed?

269. Has a resource management plan been created?

270. Do all stakeholders know how to access this repository and where to find the EDR Privileged Access Management project documentation?

271. Quality assurance overheads?

272. Has the business need been clearly defined?

273. Is the ims development and management approach described?

274. Is the schedule updated on a periodic basis?

2.11 Activity List: EDR Privileged Access Management

275. The wbs is developed as part of a joint planning session. and how do you know that you have done this right?

276. How do you determine the late start (LS) for each activity?

277. For other activities, how much delay can be tolerated?

278. How can the EDR Privileged Access Management project be displayed graphically to better visualize the activities?

279. What are the critical bottleneck activities?

280. What did not go as well?

281. Is infrastructure setup part of your EDR Privileged Access Management project?

282. How much slack is available in the EDR Privileged Access Management project?

283. What is your organizations history in doing similar activities?

284. When do the individual activities need to start and finish?

285. Who will perform the work?

286. When will the work be performed?

287. Where will it be performed?

288. What is the LF and LS for each activity?

289. Are the required resources available or need to be acquired?

290. How should ongoing costs be monitored to try to keep the EDR Privileged Access Management project within budget?

291. How will it be performed?

292. In what sequence?

2.12 Activity Attributes: EDR Privileged Access Management

293. Activity: fair or not fair?

294. How many days do you need to complete the work scope with a limit of X number of resources?

295. What activity do you think you should spend the most time on?

296. Does your organization of the data change its meaning?

297. Have constraints been applied to the start and finish milestones for the phases?

298. Have you identified the Activity Leveling Priority code value on each activity?

299. Resources to accomplish the work?

300. What conclusions/generalizations can you draw from this?

301. Is there a trend during the year?

302. How else could the items be grouped?

303. Has management defined a definite timeframe for the turnaround or EDR Privileged Access Management project window?

304. Are the required resources available?

305. Why?

306. Would you consider either of corresponding activities an outlier?

307. Were there other ways you could have organized the data to achieve similar results?

308. How difficult will it be to complete specific activities on this EDR Privileged Access Management project?

309. Where else does it apply?

2.13 Milestone List: EDR Privileged Access Management

310. What is the market for your technology, product or service?

311. How late can the activity finish?

312. What date will the task finish?

313. Political effects?

314. Environmental effects?

315. What are your competitors vulnerabilities?

316. Information and research?

317. Loss of key staff?

318. Continuity, supply chain robustness?

319. Effects on core activities, distraction?

320. Obstacles faced?

321. Identify critical paths (one or more) and which activities are on the critical path?

322. Milestone pages should display the UserID of the person who added the milestone. Does a report or query exist that provides this audit information?

323. Marketing - reach, distribution, awareness?

324. Timescales, deadlines and pressures?

325. Sustaining internal capabilities?

326. When will the EDR Privileged Access Management project be complete?

327. How will the milestone be verified?

2.14 Network Diagram: EDR Privileged Access Management

328. If a current contract exists, can you provide the vendor name, contract start, and contract expiration date?

329. Are you on time?

330. What controls the start and finish of a job?

331. Review the logical flow of the network diagram. Take a look at which activities you have first and then sequence the activities. Do they make sense?

332. What job or jobs could run concurrently?

333. What to do and When?

334. How confident can you be in your milestone dates and the delivery date?

335. Where do you schedule uncertainty time?

336. What activity must be completed immediately before this activity can start?

337. Exercise: what is the probability that the EDR Privileged Access Management project duration will exceed xx weeks?

338. Can you calculate the confidence level?

339. How difficult will it be to do specific activities on this EDR Privileged Access Management project?

340. What can be done concurrently?

341. Planning: who, how long, what to do?

342. What job or jobs precede it?

343. What is the completion time?

344. Which type of network diagram allows you to depict four types of dependencies?

345. What are the Major Administrative Issues?

2.15 Activity Resource Requirements: EDR Privileged Access Management

346. Time for overtime?

347. How many signatures do you require on a check and does this match what is in your policy and procedures?

348. Is there anything planned that does not need to be here?

349. Do you use tools like decomposition and rolling-wave planning to produce the activity list and other outputs?

350. What is the Work Plan Standard?

351. Other support in specific areas?

352. When does monitoring begin?

353. Are there unresolved issues that need to be addressed?

354. Why do you do that?

355. Organizational Applicability?

356. Anything else?

357. What are constraints that you might find during the Human Resource Planning process?

358. How do you handle petty cash?

359. Which logical relationship does the PDM use most often?

2.16 Resource Breakdown Structure: EDR Privileged Access Management

360. Why is this important?

361. Is predictive resource analysis being done?

362. How difficult will it be to do specific activities on this EDR Privileged Access Management project?

363. What is the primary purpose of the human resource plan?

364. What is the purpose of assigning and documenting responsibility?

365. Which resources should be in the resource pool?

366. Goals for the EDR Privileged Access Management project. What is each stakeholders desired outcome for the EDR Privileged Access Management project?

367. Who will use the system?

368. Who needs what information?

369. When do they need the information?

370. What are the requirements for resource data?

371. What is EDR Privileged Access Management project communication management?

372. Who delivers the information?

373. What can you do to improve productivity?

374. Which resource planning tool provides information on resource responsibility and accountability?

375. What is the difference between % Complete and % work?

376. The list could probably go on, but, the thing that you would most like to know is, How long & How much?

2.17 Activity Duration Estimates: EDR Privileged Access Management

377. Is the EDR Privileged Access Management project performing better or worse than planned?

378. What is earned value?

379. Do an internet search on earning pmp certification. be sure to search for yahoo groups related to this topic. what are the options you found to help people prepare for the exam?

380. It under budget or over budget?

381. Are procedures defined by which the EDR Privileged Access Management project scope may be changed?

382. How does EDR Privileged Access Management project management relate to other disciplines?

383. List five reasons why organizations outsource. Why is there a growing trend in outsourcing, especially in the government?

384. Is a provider selected based upon defined evaluation criteria?

385. Does a process exist to formally recognize new EDR Privileged Access Management projects?

386. Are steps identified by which EDR Privileged

Access Management project documents may be changed?

387. Are team building activities completed to improve team performance?

388. What should be done NEXT?

389. How difficult will it be to do specific activities on this EDR Privileged Access Management project?

390. Why time management?

391. Are EDR Privileged Access Management project activities decomposed into manageable components to ensure expected management control?

392. Are performance reviews conducted regularly to assess the status of EDR Privileged Access Management projects?

393. How does poking fun at technical professionals communications skills impact the industry and educational programs?

394. Are risks that are likely to affect the EDR Privileged Access Management project identified and documented?

395. Which skills do you think are most important for an information technology EDR Privileged Access Management project manager?

396. Are inspections completed to determine if the results comply with the requirements?

2.18 Duration Estimating Worksheet: EDR Privileged Access Management

397. What work will be included in the EDR Privileged Access Management project?

398. What is cost and EDR Privileged Access Management project cost management?

399. What is next?

400. What questions do you have?

401. Why estimate time and cost?

402. Is a construction detail attached (to aid in explanation)?

403. How should ongoing costs be monitored to try to keep the EDR Privileged Access Management project within budget?

404. Is this operation cost effective?

405. When, then?

406. Science = process: remember the scientific method?

407. Done before proceeding with this activity or what can be done concurrently?

408. What utility impacts are there?

409. Is the EDR Privileged Access Management project responsive to community need?

410. Will the EDR Privileged Access Management project collaborate with the local community and leverage resources?

411. When does your organization expect to be able to complete it?

412. Do any colleagues have experience with your organization and/or RFPs?

413. Does the EDR Privileged Access Management project provide innovative ways for stakeholders to overcome obstacles or deliver better outcomes?

2.19 Project Schedule: EDR Privileged Access Management

414. Is there a Schedule Management Plan that establishes the criteria and activities for developing, monitoring and controlling the EDR Privileged Access Management project schedule?

415. Change management required?

416. Verify that the update is accurate. Are all remaining durations correct?

417. Why or why not?

418. What is EDR Privileged Access Management project management?

419. Why do you need schedules?

420. If you can not fix it, how do you do it differently?

421. How do you manage EDR Privileged Access Management project Risk?

422. To what degree is do you feel the entire team was committed to the EDR Privileged Access Management project schedule?

423. Schedule/cost recovery?

424. How does a EDR Privileged Access Management project get to be a year late ?

425. What does that mean?

426. Meet requirements?

427. How can you shorten the schedule?

428. Understand the constraints used in preparing the schedule. Are activities connected because logic dictates the order in which others occur?

429. Why do you think schedule issues often cause the most conflicts on EDR Privileged Access Management projects?

430. What is the most mis-scheduled part of process?

431. Is infrastructure setup part of your EDR Privileged Access Management project?

432. Is the EDR Privileged Access Management project schedule available for all EDR Privileged Access Management project team members to review?

2.20 Cost Management Plan: EDR Privileged Access Management

433. Is the assigned EDR Privileged Access Management project manager a PMP (Certified EDR Privileged Access Management project manager) and experienced?

434. Has your organization readiness assessment been conducted?

435. Are mitigation strategies identified?

436. Schedule variances – how will schedule variances be identified and corrected?

437. Are internal EDR Privileged Access Management project status meetings held at reasonable intervals?

438. Are enough systems & user personnel assigned to the EDR Privileged Access Management project?

439. Is an industry recognized mechanized support tool(s) being used for EDR Privileged Access Management project scheduling & tracking?

440. For cost control purposes?

441. Scope of work – What is the likelihood and extent of potential future changes to the EDR Privileged Access Management project scope?

442. Sensitivity analysis?

443. Is the EDR Privileged Access Management project sponsor clearly communicating the business case or rationale for why this EDR Privileged Access Management project is needed?

444. Have activity relationships and interdependencies within tasks been adequately identified?

445. Why do you manage cost?

446. Mitigation – based on the action, cost and probability of success, will the mitigation be made?

447. Were stakeholders aware and supportive of the principles and practices of modern software estimation?

448. How difficult will it be to do specific tasks on the EDR Privileged Access Management project?

449. Is your organization certified as a supplier, wholesaler and/or regular dealer?

450. Personnel with expertise?

451. Cost tracking and performance analysis – How will cost tracking and performance analysis be accomplished?

2.21 Activity Cost Estimates: EDR Privileged Access Management

452. How Award?

453. Review – what are some common errors in activities to avoid?

454. Is there anything unique in this EDR Privileged Access Management projects scope statement that will affect resources?

455. Who & what determines the need for contracted services?

456. Was it performed on time?

457. Does the activity serve a common type of customer?

458. How quickly can the task be done with the skills available?

459. What is included in indirect cost being allocated?

460. Estimated cost?

461. How many activities should you have?

462. Are cost subtotals needed?

463. How do you fund change orders?

464. Can you change your activities?

465. How difficult will it be to do specific tasks on the EDR Privileged Access Management project?

466. How do you manage cost?

467. Was the consultant knowledgeable about the program?

468. How do you allocate indirect costs to activities?

469. Who determines the quality and expertise of contractors?

470. What is the estimators estimating history?

2.22 Cost Estimating Worksheet: EDR Privileged Access Management

471. Is the EDR Privileged Access Management project responsive to community need?

472. Will the EDR Privileged Access Management project collaborate with the local community and leverage resources?

473. How will the results be shared and to whom?

474. What is the estimated labor cost today based upon this information?

475. Value pocket identification & quantification what are value pockets?

476. Can a trend be established from historical performance data on the selected measure and are the criteria for using trend analysis or forecasting methods met?

477. Ask: are others positioned to know, are others credible, and will others cooperate?

478. What can be included?

479. What additional EDR Privileged Access Management project(s) could be initiated as a result of this EDR Privileged Access Management project?

480. Is it feasible to establish a control group

arrangement?

481. Identify the timeframe necessary to monitor progress and collect data to determine how the selected measure has changed?

482. What will others want?

483. What info is needed?

484. Does the EDR Privileged Access Management project provide innovative ways for stakeholders to overcome obstacles or deliver better outcomes?

485. Who is best positioned to know and assist in identifying corresponding factors?

486. What is the purpose of estimating?

487. What costs are to be estimated?

488. What happens to any remaining funds not used?

2.23 Cost Baseline: EDR Privileged Access Management

489. What deliverables come first?

490. Is request in line with priorities?

491. Should a more thorough impact analysis be conducted?

492. Has the actual cost of the EDR Privileged Access Management project (or EDR Privileged Access Management project phase) been tallied and compared to the approved budget?

493. Does it impact schedule, cost, quality?

494. What can go wrong?

495. On time?

496. What is the consequence?

497. Escalation criteria met?

498. Is the requested change request a result of changes in other EDR Privileged Access Management project(s)?

499. What would the life cycle costs be?

500. Vac -variance at completion, how much over/ under budget do you expect to be?

501. What is the most important thing to do next to make your EDR Privileged Access Management project successful?

502. Has the EDR Privileged Access Management projected annual cost to operate and maintain the product(s) or service(s) been approved and funded?

503. Are you meeting with your team regularly?

504. Have all approved changes to the EDR Privileged Access Management project requirement been identified and impact on the performance, cost, and schedule baselines documented?

505. Has operations management formally accepted responsibility for operating and maintaining the product(s) or service(s) delivered by the EDR Privileged Access Management project?

506. What is it ?

2.24 Quality Management Plan: EDR Privileged Access Management

507. How are new requirements or changes to requirements identified?

508. Can you perform this task or activity in a more effective manner?

509. Is the process working, and people are not executing in compliance of the process?

510. What are your organizations key processes (product, service, business, and support)?

511. What key performance indicators does your organization use to measure, manage, and improve key processes?

512. How are calibration records kept?

513. How effectively was the Quality Management Plan applied during EDR Privileged Access Management project Execution?

514. What would be the next steps or what else should you do at this point?

515. What process do you use to minimize errors, defects, and rework?

516. Who is responsible for approving the qapp?

517. What field records are generated?

518. Diagrams and tables to account for complex concepts and increase overall readability?

519. Does the system design reflect the requirements?

520. How does the material compare to a regulatory threshold?

521. What are your results for key measures/indicators of accomplishment of organizational strategy?

522. How is staff trained in procedures?

523. Were the right locations/samples tested for the right parameters?

524. How does your organization manage work to promote cooperation, individual initiative, innovation, flexibility, communications, and knowledge/skill sharing across work units?

525. Modifications to the requirements?

526. What procedures are used to determine if you use, and the number of split, replicate or duplicate samples taken at a site?

2.25 Quality Metrics: EDR Privileged Access Management

527. How are requirements conflicts resolved?

528. Are applicable standards referenced and available?

529. If the defect rate during testing is substantially higher than that of the previous release (or a similar product), then ask: Did you plan for and actually improve testing effectiveness?

530. What is the CMS Benchmark?

531. What is the timeline to meet your goal?

532. What group is empowered to define quality requirements?

533. Are quality metrics defined?

534. How do you calculate corresponding metrics?

535. Are there already quality metrics available that detect nonlinear embeddings and trends similar to the users perception?

536. How do you communicate results and findings to upper management?

537. What is the benchmark?

538. Is there a set of procedures to capture, analyze and act on quality metrics?

539. How can the effectiveness of each of the activities be measured?

540. Is the reporting frequency appropriate?

541. Should a modifier be included?

542. Which are the right metrics to use?

543. Is quality culture a competitive advantage?

544. Did the team meet the EDR Privileged Access Management project success criteria documented in the Quality Metrics Matrix?

545. Are interface issues coordinated?

2.26 Process Improvement Plan: EDR Privileged Access Management

546. Why do you want to achieve the goal?

547. How do you measure?

548. Has a process guide to collect the data been developed?

549. Are you making progress on the goals?

550. Everyone agrees on what process improvement is, right?

551. What actions are needed to address the problems and achieve the goals?

552. Are there forms and procedures to collect and record the data?

553. How do you manage quality?

554. To elicit goal statements, do you ask a question such as, What do you want to achieve?

555. Who should prepare the process improvement action plan?

556. Where do you want to be?

557. If a process improvement framework is being used, which elements will help the problems and

goals listed?

558. What is the return on investment?

559. Are you making progress on the improvement framework?

560. Where do you focus?

561. What personnel are the change agents for your initiative?

562. Modeling current processes is great, and will you ever see a return on that investment?

563. What is quality and how will you ensure it?

564. Have storage and access mechanisms and procedures been determined?

2.27 Responsibility Assignment Matrix: EDR Privileged Access Management

565. What simple tool can you use to help identify and prioritize EDR Privileged Access Management project risks that is very low tech and high touch?

566. Does the EDR Privileged Access Management project need to be analyzed further to uncover additional responsibilities?

567. Are there any drawbacks to using a responsibility assignment matrix?

568. Are others working on the right things?

569. Are records maintained to show how management reserves are used?

570. What are the assumptions?

571. Cwbs elements to be subcontracted, with identification of subcontractors?

572. Which EDR Privileged Access Management project management knowledge area is least mature?

573. Changes in the current direct and EDR Privileged Access Management projected base?

574. Is every signing-off responsibility and every communicating responsibility critically necessary?

575. Actual cost of work performed?

576. Too many is: do all the identified roles need to be routinely informed or only in exceptional circumstances?

577. Changes in the nature of the overhead requirements?

578. Direct labor dollars and/or hours?

579. Will too many Signing-off responsibilities delay the completion of the activity/deliverable?

580. Changes in the direct base to which overhead costs are allocated?

581. Wbs elements contractually specified for reporting of status (lowest level only)?

582. Do you know how your people are allocated?

2.28 Roles and Responsibilities: EDR Privileged Access Management

583. What specific behaviors did you observe?

584. Are governance roles and responsibilities documented?

585. What should you do now to ensure that you are exceeding expectations and excelling in your current position?

586. How is your work-life balance?

587. Who is involved?

588. Are your policies supportive of a culture of quality data?

589. Does the team have access to and ability to use data analysis tools?

590. What areas would you highlight for changes or improvements?

591. To decide whether to use a quality measurement, ask how will you know when it is achieved?

592. What expectations were met?

593. What should you highlight for improvement?

594. What expectations were NOT met?

595. What is working well within your organizations performance management system?

596. Does your vision/mission support a culture of quality data?

597. Authority: what areas/EDR Privileged Access Management projects in your work do you have the authority to decide upon and act on the already stated decisions?

598. Who: who is involved?

599. What is working well?

600. Do you take the time to clearly define roles and responsibilities on EDR Privileged Access Management project tasks?

601. Once the responsibilities are defined for the EDR Privileged Access Management project, have the deliverables, roles and responsibilities been clearly communicated to every participant?

2.29 Human Resource Management Plan: EDR Privileged Access Management

602. Are key risk mitigation strategies added to the EDR Privileged Access Management project schedule?

603. What were things that you did very well and want to do the same again on the next EDR Privileged Access Management project?

604. Are action items captured and managed?

605. Is there a formal process for updating the EDR Privileged Access Management project baseline?

606. Were stakeholders aware and supportive of the principles and practices of modern cost estimation?

607. Has the EDR Privileged Access Management project manager been identified?

608. Are internal EDR Privileged Access Management project status meetings held at reasonable intervals?

609. Has a provision been made to reassess EDR Privileged Access Management project risks at various EDR Privileged Access Management project stages?

610. Was the EDR Privileged Access Management project schedule reviewed by all stakeholders and formally accepted?

611. Is there any form of automated support for Issues Management?

612. Is stakeholder involvement adequate?

613. How are superior performers differentiated from average performers?

614. Are all key components of a Quality Assurance Plan present?

615. Is it standard practice to formally commit stakeholders to the EDR Privileged Access Management project via agreements?

616. Cost / benefit analysis?

617. Are the appropriate IT resources adequate to meet planned commitments?

618. Have EDR Privileged Access Management project management standards and procedures been identified / established and documented?

619. Who needs training?

620. Are enough systems & user personnel assigned to the EDR Privileged Access Management project?

2.30 Communications Management Plan: EDR Privileged Access Management

621. What help do you and your team need from the stakeholder?

622. Can you think of other people who might have concerns or interests?

623. Who is the stakeholder?

624. Are others part of the communications management plan?

625. Do you feel a register helps?

626. How will the person responsible for executing the communication item be notified?

627. Why is stakeholder engagement important?

628. Which team member will work with each stakeholder?

629. Who to learn from?

630. Are there potential barriers between the team and the stakeholder?

631. What to know?

632. What approaches do you use?

633. What is the stakeholders level of authority?

634. How much time does it take to do it?

635. Do you ask; can you recommend others for you to talk with about this initiative?

636. Are you constantly rushing from meeting to meeting?

637. Do you prepare stakeholder engagement plans?

638. What are the interrelationships?

2.31 Risk Management Plan: EDR Privileged Access Management

639. Have you worked with the customer in the past?

640. Do you manage the process through use of metrics?

641. Which risks should get the attention?

642. Is a software EDR Privileged Access Management project management tool available?

643. Is the process supported by tools?

644. How well were you able to manage your risk before?

645. Are some people working on multiple EDR Privileged Access Management projects?

646. Are there risks to human health or the environment that need to be controlled or mitigated?

647. What risks are tracked?

648. What should be done with non-critical risks?

649. Are you on schedule?

650. Was an original risk assessment/risk management plan completed?

651. Why do you want risk management?

652. Are tool mentors available?

653. Should the risk be taken at all?

654. Technology risk: is the EDR Privileged Access Management project technically feasible?

655. What are the chances the event will occur?

656. Do end-users have realistic expectations?

657. Internal technical and management reviews?

2.32 Risk Register: EDR Privileged Access Management

658. What is a Community Risk Register?

659. What may happen or not go according to plan?

660. What is the reason for current performance gaps and do the risks and opportunities identified previously account for this?

661. People risk -are people with appropriate skills available to help complete the EDR Privileged Access Management project?

662. How are risks graded?

663. Who is going to do it?

664. What further options might be available for responding to the risk?

665. What evidence do you have to justify the likelihood score of the risk (audit, incident report, claim, complaints, inspection, internal review)?

666. Schedule impact/severity estimated range (workdays) assume the event happens, what is the potential impact?

667. What can be done about it?

668. Are corrective measures implemented as

planned?

669. What has changed since the last period?

670. How could corresponding Risk affect the EDR Privileged Access Management project in terms of cost and schedule?

671. Can the likelihood and impact of failing to achieve corresponding recommendations and action plans be assessed?

672. Does the evidence highlight any areas to advance opportunities or foster good relations. If yes what steps will be taken?

673. Are your objectives at risk?

674. Is further information required before making a decision?

675. Cost/benefit – how much will the proposed mitigations cost and how does this cost compare with the potential cost of the risk event/situation should it occur?

676. Having taken action, how did the responses effect change, and where is the EDR Privileged Access Management project now?

2.33 Probability and Impact Assessment: EDR Privileged Access Management

677. Anticipated volatility of the requirements?

678. Can the EDR Privileged Access Management project proceed without assuming the risk?

679. What is the impact if the risk does occur?

680. Has the need for the EDR Privileged Access Management project been properly established?

681. Can you avoid altogether some things that might go wrong?

682. Does the software engineering team have the right mix of skills?

683. Is security a central objective?

684. Do requirements demand the use of new analysis, design, or testing methods?

685. What are the uncertainties associated with the technology selected for the EDR Privileged Access Management project?

686. Is the customer willing to commit significant time to the requirements gathering process?

687. Are enough people available?

688. How realistic is the timing of introduction?

689. What is the probability of the risk occurring?

690. How is the EDR Privileged Access Management project going to be managed?

691. Which risks need to move on to Perform Quantitative Risk Analysis?

692. Are testing tools available and suitable?

693. My EDR Privileged Access Management project leader has suddenly left your organization, what do you do?

694. What significant shift will occur in governmental policies, laws, and regulations pertaining to specific industries?

695. Which of your EDR Privileged Access Management projects should be selected when compared with other EDR Privileged Access Management projects?

696. Risk may be made during which step of risk management?

2.34 Probability and Impact Matrix: EDR Privileged Access Management

697. What should be done with risks on the watch list?

698. What do you expect?

699. How much risk do others need to take?

700. Which should be probably done NEXT?

701. Sensitivity analysis -which risks will have the most impact on the EDR Privileged Access Management project?

702. What risks are necessary to achieve success?

703. Are the software tools integrated with each other?

704. Are some people working on multiple EDR Privileged Access Management projects?

705. What will be cost of redeployment of the personnel?

706. Have staff received necessary training?

707. How is the risk management process used in practice?

708. What are the uncertainties associated with the technology selected for the EDR Privileged Access

Management project?

709. Do you train all developers in the process?

710. What are the current requirements of the customer?

711. Is the number of people on the EDR Privileged Access Management project team adequate to do the job?

712. Mandated specific features?

713. Have customers been involved fully in the definition of requirements?

714. How to prioritize risks?

715. Is the customer willing to establish rapid communication links with the developer?

2.35 Risk Data Sheet: EDR Privileged Access Management

716. What are your core values?

717. What is the chance that it will happen?

718. Has a sensitivity analysis been carried out?

719. Potential for recurrence?

720. What are you trying to achieve (Objectives)?

721. What will be the consequences if the risk happens?

722. What were the Causes that contributed?

723. What actions can be taken to eliminate or remove risk?

724. What are you here for (Mission)?

725. Whom do you serve (customers)?

726. What can happen?

727. Are new hazards created?

728. Will revised controls lead to tolerable risk levels?

729. What are the main opportunities available to you that you should grab while you can?

730. What can you do?

731. What was measured?

732. What are you weak at and therefore need to do better?

733. Type of risk identified?

2.36 Procurement Management Plan: EDR Privileged Access Management

734. Are meeting minutes captured and sent out after meetings?

735. Are key risk mitigation strategies added to the EDR Privileged Access Management project schedule?

736. Are cause and effect determined for risks when others occur?

737. Have the key elements of a coherent EDR Privileged Access Management project management strategy been established?

738. Has a capability assessment been conducted?

739. Are assumptions being identified, recorded, analyzed, qualified and closed?

740. Does the EDR Privileged Access Management project team have the right skills?

741. Are actuals compared against estimates to analyze and correct variances?

742. Are the EDR Privileged Access Management project plans updated on a frequent basis?

743. How long will it take for the purchase cost to be the same as the lease cost?

744. Are any non-compliance issues that exist communicated to your organization?

745. Is the steering committee active in EDR Privileged Access Management project oversight?

746. Is the assigned EDR Privileged Access Management project manager a PMP (Certified EDR Privileged Access Management project manager) and experienced?

747. Are EDR Privileged Access Management project leaders committed to this EDR Privileged Access Management project full time?

748. Have key stakeholders been identified?

749. Has the schedule been baselined?

750. Has the EDR Privileged Access Management project scope been baselined?

751. Have stakeholder accountabilities & responsibilities been clearly defined?

2.37 Source Selection Criteria: EDR Privileged Access Management

752. How will you evaluate offerors proposals?

753. In the technical/management area, what criteria do you use to determine the final evaluation ratings?

754. What is the effect of the debriefing schedule on potential protests?

755. How are clarifications and communications appropriately used?

756. Are there any specific considerations that precludes offers from being selected as the awardee?

757. Are evaluators ready to begin this task?

758. What information may not be provided?

759. Are responses to considerations adequate?

760. Who is on the Source Selection Advisory Committee?

761. Is there collaboration among your evaluators?

762. In which phase of the acquisition process cycle does source qualifications reside?

763. Does your documentation identify why the team concurs or differs with reported performance

from past performance report (CPARs, questionnaire responses, etc.)?

764. What are the guiding principles for developing an evaluation report?

765. What should be the contracting officers strategy?

766. What instructions should be provided regarding oral presentations?

767. How should oral presentations be prepared for?

768. How do you manage procurement?

769. What should a DRFP include?

770. How can the methods of publicizing the buy be tailored to yield more effective price competition?

771. What benefits are accrued from issuing a DRFP in advance of issuing a final RFP?

2.38 Stakeholder Management Plan: EDR Privileged Access Management

772. What is meant by activity dependencies and how do they relate to network diagramming?

773. Have all involved stakeholders and work groups committed to the EDR Privileged Access Management project?

774. Is the quality assurance team identified?

775. Are the EDR Privileged Access Management project team members located locally to the users/ stakeholders?

776. Are formal code reviews conducted?

777. Have reserves been created to address risks?

778. Are there checklists created to demine if all quality processes are followed?

779. Is there an issues management plan in place?

780. Are software metrics formally captured, analyzed and used as a basis for other EDR Privileged Access Management project estimates?

781. Who might be involved in developing a charter?

782. What action will be taken once reports have been received?

783. What are the procedures and processes to be followed for purchases, including approval and authorisation requirements?

784. Alignment to strategic goals & objectives?

785. What are the criteria for selecting suppliers of off the shelf products?

786. Has a sponsor been identified?

2.39 Change Management Plan: EDR Privileged Access Management

787. What are the major changes to processes?

788. What roles within your organization are affected, and how?

789. Has the target training audience been identified and nominated?

790. What skills, education, knowledge, or work experiences should the resources have for each identified competency?

791. Why is the initiative is being undertaken - What are the business drivers?

792. Has a training need analysis been carried out?

793. What are the essentials of the message?

794. Have the business unit contacts been briefed by the EDR Privileged Access Management project team?

795. Who might present the most resistance?

796. Who is the target audience of the piece of information?

797. Where will the funds come from?

798. How badly can information be misinterpreted?

799. When does it make sense to customize?

800. What are the current methods of sharing information and do there need to be new ones developed?

801. Identify the risk and assess the significance and likelihood of it occurring and plan the contingency What risks may occur upfront?

802. What new behaviours are required?

803. Do the proposed users have access to the appropriate documentation?

804. Why would a EDR Privileged Access Management project run more smoothly when change management is emphasized from the beginning?

3.0 Executing Process Group: EDR Privileged Access Management

805. What is involved in the solicitation process?

806. What are the critical steps involved with strategy mapping?

807. What are some crucial elements of a good EDR Privileged Access Management project plan?

808. What were things that you did very well and want to do the same again on the next EDR Privileged Access Management project?

809. How will you know you did it?

810. Is activity definition the first process involved in EDR Privileged Access Management project time management?

811. What are the EDR Privileged Access Management project management deliverables of each process group?

812. What were things that you did well, and could improve, and how?

813. What are crucial elements of successful EDR Privileged Access Management project plan execution?

814. How will professionals learn what is expected

from them what the deliverables are?

815. How could stakeholders negatively impact your EDR Privileged Access Management project?

816. How will you avoid scope creep?

817. What are the critical steps involved in selecting measures and initiatives?

818. Specific - is the objective clear in terms of what, how, when, and where the situation will be changed?

819. Does software appear easy to learn?

820. Does the EDR Privileged Access Management project team have enough people to execute the EDR Privileged Access Management project plan?

821. In what way has the program come up with innovative measures for problem-solving?

822. What will you do to minimize the impact should a risk event occur?

3.1 Team Member Status Report: EDR Privileged Access Management

823. Why is it to be done?

824. Does your organization have the means (staff, money, contract, etc.) to produce or to acquire the product, good, or service?

825. Do you have an Enterprise EDR Privileged Access Management project Management Office (EPMO)?

826. Are the attitudes of staff regarding EDR Privileged Access Management project work improving?

827. What specific interest groups do you have in place?

828. Does every department have to have a EDR Privileged Access Management project Manager on staff?

829. Are your organizations EDR Privileged Access Management projects more successful over time?

830. Is there evidence that staff is taking a more professional approach toward management of your organizations EDR Privileged Access Management projects?

831. When a teams productivity and success depend on collaboration and the efficient flow of information, what generally fails them?

832. Does the product, good, or service already exist within your organization?

833. Are the products of your organizations EDR Privileged Access Management projects meeting customers objectives?

834. How does this product, good, or service meet the needs of the EDR Privileged Access Management project and your organization as a whole?

835. How it is to be done?

836. What is to be done?

837. The problem with Reward & Recognition Programs is that the truly deserving people all too often get left out. How can you make it practical?

838. Will the staff do training or is that done by a third party?

839. How will resource planning be done?

840. How can you make it practical?

841. How much risk is involved?

3.2 Change Request: EDR Privileged Access Management

842. What must be taken into consideration when introducing change control programs?

843. How are changes graded and who is responsible for the rating?

844. How can changes be graded?

845. What should be regulated in a change control operating instruction?

846. Why do you want to have a change control system?

847. Should staff call into the helpdesk or go to the website?

848. How shall the implementation of changes be recorded?

849. How are changes requested (forms, method of communication)?

850. Are change requests logged and managed?

851. Who is responsible for the implementation and monitoring of all measures?

852. Describe how modifications, enhancements, defects and/or deficiencies shall be notified (e.g.

Problem Reports, Change Requests etc) and managed. Detail warranty and/or maintenance periods?

853. What type of changes does change control take into account?

854. Can you answer what happened, who did it, when did it happen, and what else will be affected?

855. Since there are no change requests in your EDR Privileged Access Management project at this point, what must you have before you begin?

856. When do you create a change request?

857. Are there requirements attributes that are strongly related to the complexity and size?

858. For which areas does this operating procedure apply?

859. What are the duties of the change control team?

860. Change request coordination ?

861. Who is responsible to authorize changes?

3.3 Change Log: EDR Privileged Access Management

862. Is the requested change request a result of changes in other EDR Privileged Access Management project(s)?

863. Is the change backward compatible without limitations?

864. Is the change request within EDR Privileged Access Management project scope?

865. Do the described changes impact on the integrity or security of the system?

866. How does this change affect scope?

867. Will the EDR Privileged Access Management project fail if the change request is not executed?

868. Is the submitted change a new change or a modification of a previously approved change?

869. Where do changes come from?

870. When was the request submitted?

871. Does the suggested change request represent a desired enhancement to the products functionality?

872. When was the request approved?

873. Who initiated the change request?

874. Is this a mandatory replacement?

875. Is the change request open, closed or pending?

876. How does this relate to the standards developed for specific business processes?

877. How does this change affect the timeline of the schedule?

878. Does the suggested change request seem to represent a necessary enhancement to the product?

3.4 Decision Log: EDR Privileged Access Management

879. How do you define success?

880. Who is the decisionmaker?

881. What makes you different or better than others companies selling the same thing?

882. With whom was the decision shared or considered?

883. Which variables make a critical difference?

884. Is everything working as expected?

885. What is the line where eDiscovery ends and document review begins?

886. How does the use a Decision Support System influence the strategies/tactics or costs?

887. How do you know when you are achieving it?

888. At what point in time does loss become unacceptable?

889. What are the cost implications?

890. Decision-making process; how will the team make decisions?

891. Adversarial environment. is your opponent open to a non-traditional workflow, or will it likely challenge anything you do?

892. What is the average size of your matters in an applicable measurement?

893. Do strategies and tactics aimed at less than full control reduce the costs of management or simply shift the cost burden?

894. Who will be given a copy of this document and where will it be kept?

895. What was the rationale for the decision?

896. How effective is maintaining the log at facilitating organizational learning?

897. What alternatives/risks were considered?

898. Meeting purpose; why does this team meet?

3.5 Quality Audit: EDR Privileged Access Management

899. How does your organization know that its management of its ethical responsibilities is appropriately effective and constructive?

900. Does the report read coherently?

901. How are you auditing your organizations compliance with regulations?

902. Will the evidence likely be sufficient and appropriate?

903. For each device to be reconditioned, are device specifications, such as appropriate engineering drawings, component specifications and software specifications, maintained?

904. How does your organization know that its systems for communicating with and among staff are appropriately effective and constructive?

905. How does your organization know that the quality of its supervisors is appropriately effective and constructive?

906. How does your organization know that its system for inducting new staff to maximize workplace contributions are appropriately effective and constructive?

907. How does your organization know that its system for managing intellectual property issues is appropriately effective, constructive and fair?

908. How does your organization know that its relationships with the community at large are appropriately effective and constructive?

909. How does your organization know that its system for recruiting the best staff possible are appropriately effective and constructive?

910. Are complaint files maintained?

911. How does your organization know that the range and quality of its accommodation, catering and transportation services are appropriately effective and constructive?

912. How does your organization know that its research planning and management systems are appropriately effective and constructive in enabling quality research outcomes?

913. How does your organization know that the support for its staff is appropriately effective and constructive?

914. How does your organization know that its relationship with its (past) staff is appropriately effective and constructive?

915. How does your organization know that its processes for managing severance are appropriately effective, constructive and fair?

916. Is quality audit a prerequisite for program accreditation or program recognition?

917. What mechanisms exist for identification of staff development needs?

3.6 Team Directory: EDR Privileged Access Management

918. Process decisions: do job conditions warrant additional actions to collect job information and document on-site activity?

919. Where will the product be used and/or delivered or built when appropriate?

920. Why is the work necessary?

921. When does information need to be distributed?

922. Process decisions: are there any statutory or regulatory issues relevant to the timely execution of work?

923. Process decisions: are all start-up, turn over and close out requirements of the contract satisfied?

924. Where should the information be distributed?

925. Does a EDR Privileged Access Management project team directory list all resources assigned to the EDR Privileged Access Management project?

926. Who will talk to the customer?

927. Have you decided when to celebrate the EDR Privileged Access Management projects completion date?

928. Process decisions: how well was task order work performed?

929. How will the team handle changes?

930. How does the team resolve conflicts and ensure tasks are completed?

931. Who are the Team Members?

932. Timing: when do the effects of communication take place?

933. Process decisions: do invoice amounts match accepted work in place?

934. How do unidentified risks impact the outcome of the EDR Privileged Access Management project?

3.7 Team Operating Agreement: EDR Privileged Access Management

935. Did you draft the meeting agenda?

936. Are there influences outside the team that may affect performance, and if so, have you identified and addressed them?

937. How will your group handle planned absences?

938. What are the current caseload numbers in the unit?

939. What is the number of cases currently teamed?

940. Do you prevent individuals from dominating the meeting?

941. Do you vary your voice pace, tone and pitch to engage participants and gain involvement?

942. Do you ensure that all participants know how to use the required technology?

943. What is group supervision?

944. Do you post meeting notes and the recording (if used) and notify participants?

945. What is your unique contribution to your organization?

946. Do you listen for voice tone and word choice to understand the meaning behind words?

947. How will group handle unplanned absences?

948. What are the boundaries (organizational or geographic) within which you operate?

949. What went well?

950. What are the safety issues/risks that need to be addressed and/or that the team needs to consider?

951. To whom do you deliver your services?

952. Have you set the goals and objectives of the team?

953. Do you brief absent members after they view meeting notes or listen to a recording?

954. Has the appropriate access to relevant data and analysis capability been granted?

3.8 Team Performance Assessment: EDR Privileged Access Management

955. To what degree does the teams purpose constitute a broader, deeper aspiration than just accomplishing short-term goals?

956. Is there a particular method of data analysis that you would recommend as a means of demonstrating that method variance is not of great concern for a given dataset?

957. Where to from here?

958. Do friends perform better than acquaintances?

959. Do you give group members authority to make at least some important decisions?

960. Which situations call for a more extreme type of adaptiveness in which team members actually re-define roles?

961. What do you think is the most constructive thing that could be done now to resolve considerations and disputes about method variance?

962. To what degree do team members articulate the teams work approach?

963. How hard did you try to make a good selection?

964. To what degree can team members frequently

and easily communicate with one another?

965. To what degree do team members agree with the goals, relative importance, and the ways in which achievement will be measured?

966. To what degree will the approach capitalize on and enhance the skills of all team members in a manner that takes into consideration other demands on members of the team?

967. Can team performance be reliably measured in simulator and live exercises using the same assessment tool?

968. To what degree are the relative importance and priority of the goals clear to all team members?

969. To what degree is the team cognizant of small wins to be celebrated along the way?

970. How much interpersonal friction is there in your team?

971. Individual task proficiency and team process behavior: what is important for team functioning?

972. What is method variance?

973. To what degree can team members vigorously define the teams purpose in considerations with others who are not part of the functioning team?

974. To what degree are sub-teams possible or necessary?

3.9 Team Member Performance Assessment: EDR Privileged Access Management

975. Who they are?

976. Are any validation activities performed?

977. New skills/knowledge gained this year?

978. How accurately is your plan implemented?

979. How do you know that all team members are learning?

980. Why were corresponding selected?

981. What innovations (if any) are developed to realize goals?

982. How are evaluation results utilized?

983. To what degree will new and supplemental skills be introduced as the need is recognized?

984. What is the target group for instruction (e.g., individual and collective or small team instruction)?

985. To what degree can team members meet frequently enough to accomplish the teams ends?

986. How is your organizations Strategic Management System tied to performance measurement?

987. How should adaptive assessments be implemented?

988. Why do performance reviews?

989. Do the goals support your organizations goals?

990. What are the staffs preferences for training on technology-based platforms?

991. Goals met?

992. To what degree do team members feel that the purpose of the team is important, if not exciting?

993. How often should assessments be conducted?

994. Are assessment validation activities performed?

3.10 Issue Log: EDR Privileged Access Management

995. In classifying stakeholders, which approach to do so are you using?

996. Who do you turn to if you have questions?

997. Is there an important stakeholder who is actively opposed and will not receive messages?

998. Why multiple evaluators?

999. Who reported the issue?

1000. What date was the issue resolved?

1001. How were past initiatives successful?

1002. What is the status of the issue?

1003. Do you have members of your team responsible for certain stakeholders?

1004. How often do you engage with stakeholders?

1005. What steps can you take for positive relationships?

1006. What effort will a change need?

1007. What does the stakeholder need from the team?

1008. Who needs to know and how much?

1009. Why do you manage human resources?

1010. Why do you manage communications?

4.0 Monitoring and Controlling Process Group: EDR Privileged Access Management

1011. Measurable - are the targets measurable?

1012. How many more potential communications channels were introduced by the discovery of the new stakeholders?

1013. Where is the Risk in the EDR Privileged Access Management project?

1014. How is agile program management done?

1015. What are the goals of the program?

1016. What were things that you did very well and want to do the same again on the next EDR Privileged Access Management project?

1017. Is there sufficient funding available for this?

1018. How well did the team follow the chosen processes?

1019. When will the EDR Privileged Access Management project be done?

1020. How is Agile EDR Privileged Access Management project Management done?

1021. How were collaborations developed, and how

are they sustained?

1022. Is progress on outcomes due to your program?

1023. Propriety: who needs to be involved in the evaluation to be ethical?

1024. Is the schedule for the set products being met?

1025. What departments are involved in its daily operation?

1026. How well defined and documented were the EDR Privileged Access Management project management processes you chose to use?

1027. How do you monitor progress?

1028. Did it work?

1029. How is agile portfolio management done?

4.1 Project Performance Report: EDR Privileged Access Management

1030. What is the PRS?

1031. To what degree are the goals realistic?

1032. To what degree are the goals ambitious?

1033. To what degree do the structures of the formal organization motivate taskrelevant behavior and facilitate task completion?

1034. What is the degree to which rules govern information exchange between groups?

1035. To what degree do the goals specify concrete team work products?

1036. To what degree will the team adopt a concrete, clearly understood, and agreed-upon approach that will result in achievement of the teams goals?

1037. To what degree does the teams approach to its work allow for modification and improvement over time?

1038. To what degree does the information network communicate information relevant to the task?

1039. To what degree will the team ensure that all members equitably share the work essential to the success of the team?

1040. To what degree are the skill areas critical to team performance present?

1041. To what degree does the formal organization make use of individual resources and meet individual needs?

1042. How will procurement be coordinated with other EDR Privileged Access Management project aspects, such as scheduling and performance reporting?

1043. To what degree does the informal organization make use of individual resources and meet individual needs?

1044. To what degree is there a sense that only the team can succeed?

1045. To what degree are the demands of the task compatible with and converge with the mission and functions of the formal organization?

4.2 Variance Analysis: EDR Privileged Access Management

1046. How does the monthly budget compare to the actual experience?

1047. Is work properly classified as measured effort, LOE, or apportioned effort and appropriately separated?

1048. Why do variances exist?

1049. Who is generally responsible for monitoring and taking action on variances?

1050. What costs are avoidable if one or more customers are dropped?

1051. Is the anticipated (firm and potential) business base EDR Privileged Access Management projected in a rational, consistent manner?

1052. Can the relationship with problem customers be restructured so that there is a win-win situation?

1053. Contemplated overhead expenditure for each period based on the best information currently is available?

1054. What is exceptional?

1055. What was the cause of the increase in costs?

1056. The anticipated business volume?

1057. How do you evaluate the impact of schedule changes, work around, et?

1058. What types of services and expense are shared between business segments?

1059. Does the contractor use objective results, design reviews and tests to trace schedule performance?

1060. Are detailed work packages planned as far in advance as practicable?

1061. Are your organizations and items of cost assigned to each pool identified?

1062. What is the performance to date and material commitment?

1063. What is the expected future profitability of each customer?

4.3 Earned Value Status: EDR Privileged Access Management

1064. When is it going to finish?

1065. Validation is a process of ensuring that the developed system will actually achieve the stakeholders desired outcomes; Are you building the right product? What do you validate?

1066. What is the unit of forecast value?

1067. How much is it going to cost by the finish?

1068. If earned value management (EVM) is so good in determining the true status of a EDR Privileged Access Management project and EDR Privileged Access Management project its completion, why is it that hardly any one uses it in information systems related EDR Privileged Access Management projects?

1069. Are you hitting your EDR Privileged Access Management projects targets?

1070. Earned value can be used in almost any EDR Privileged Access Management project situation and in almost any EDR Privileged Access Management project environment. it may be used on large EDR Privileged Access Management projects, medium sized EDR Privileged Access Management projects, tiny EDR Privileged Access Management projects (in cut-down form), complex and simple EDR Privileged Access Management projects and in any market sector. some people, of course, know all about earned value, they have used it for years - but perhaps not as effectively as they could have?

1071. Where are your problem areas?

1072. Verification is a process of ensuring that the developed system satisfies the stakeholders agreements and specifications; Are you building the product right? What do you verify?

1073. Where is evidence-based earned value in your organization reported?

1074. How does this compare with other EDR Privileged Access Management projects?

4.4 Risk Audit: EDR Privileged Access Management

1075. Which assets are important?

1076. Does your organization communicate regularly and effectively with its members?

1077. Do you have proper induction processes for all new paid staff and volunteers who have a specific role and responsibility?

1078. Does the customer have a solid idea of what is required?

1079. Do you conduct risk assessments on all programs, activities and events?

1080. How risk averse are you?

1081. Are all managers or operators of the facility or equipment competent or qualified?

1082. What is the Board doing to assure measurement and improve outcomes and quality and reduce avoidable adverse events?

1083. Will participants be required to sign a legally counselled waiver or risk disclaimer when entering an event?

1084. Have all possible risks/hazards been identified (including injury to staff, damage to equipment, impact on others in the community)?

1085. Do industry specialists and business risk auditors enhance audit reporting accuracy?

1086. How do you compare to other jurisdictions when managing the risk of ....?

1087. What effect would a better risk management program have had?

1088. Can analytical tests provide evidence that is as strong as evidence from traditional substantive tests?

1089. What limitations do auditors face in effectively applying risk-assessment results to the risk of material misstatement measures?

1090. Do you have a clear plan for the future that describes what you want to do and how you are going to do it?

1091. The halo effect in business risk audits: can strategic risk assessment bias auditor judgment about accounting details?

1092. What does monitoring consist of?

4.5 Contractor Status Report: EDR Privileged Access Management

1093. How is risk transferred?

1094. What was the actual budget or estimated cost for your organizations services?

1095. If applicable; describe your standard schedule for new software version releases. Are new software version releases included in the standard maintenance plan?

1096. What process manages the contracts?

1097. Who can list a EDR Privileged Access Management project as organization experience, your organization or a previous employee of your organization?

1098. What is the average response time for answering a support call?

1099. Describe how often regular updates are made to the proposed solution. Are corresponding regular updates included in the standard maintenance plan?

1100. What was the final actual cost?

1101. How long have you been using the services?

1102. What are the minimum and optimal bandwidth requirements for the proposed solution?

1103. How does the proposed individual meet each requirement?

1104. What was the budget or estimated cost for your organizations services?

1105. What was the overall budget or estimated cost?

1106. Are there contractual transfer concerns?

4.6 Formal Acceptance: EDR Privileged Access Management

1107. Was the EDR Privileged Access Management project managed well?

1108. General estimate of the costs and times to complete the EDR Privileged Access Management project?

1109. What was done right?

1110. What is the Acceptance Management Process?

1111. What can you do better next time?

1112. What are the requirements against which to test, Who will execute?

1113. Does it do what EDR Privileged Access Management project team said it would?

1114. Was the EDR Privileged Access Management project goal achieved?

1115. What function(s) does it fill or meet?

1116. Do you buy-in installation services?

1117. What features, practices, and processes proved to be strengths or weaknesses?

1118. Is formal acceptance of the EDR Privileged

Access Management project product documented and distributed?

1119. Does it do what client said it would?

1120. Was the client satisfied with the EDR Privileged Access Management project results?

1121. Do you buy pre-configured systems or build your own configuration?

1122. Was the EDR Privileged Access Management project work done on time, within budget, and according to specification?

1123. Was business value realized?

1124. What lessons were learned about your EDR Privileged Access Management project management methodology?

1125. Did the EDR Privileged Access Management project achieve its MOV?

1126. Have all comments been addressed?

5.0 Closing Process Group: EDR Privileged Access Management

1127. How will staff learn how to use the deliverables?

1128. What were things that you need to improve?

1129. Were decisions made in a timely manner?

1130. Were sponsors and decision makers available when needed outside regularly scheduled meetings?

1131. Did the EDR Privileged Access Management project team have enough people to execute the EDR Privileged Access Management project plan?

1132. How will you do it?

1133. Was the schedule met?

1134. What was learned?

1135. Are there funding or time constraints?

1136. What level of risk does the proposed budget represent to the EDR Privileged Access Management project?

1137. What were the actual outcomes?

1138. How well did the chosen processes fit the needs of the EDR Privileged Access Management project?

1139. Is there a clear cause and effect between the activity and the lesson learned?

1140. When will the EDR Privileged Access Management project be done?

5.1 Procurement Audit: EDR Privileged Access Management

1141. Was the chosen procedure the most efficient and effective for the performance of the contract?

1142. Did the contracting authority verify compliance with the basic requirements of the competition?

1143. Were the documents received scrutinised for completion and adherence to stated conditions before the tenders were evaluated?

1144. Can small orders such as magazine subscriptions and non-product items such as membership in organizations be processed by the ordering department?

1145. Is there no evidence that the expert has influenced the decisions taken by the public authority in his/her interest or in the interest of a specific contractor?

1146. Are internal control mechanisms performed before payments?

1147. Are staff members evaluated in accordance with the terms of existing negotiated agreements?

1148. How do you address the risk of fraud and corruption?

1149. Audits: when was your last independent public

accountant (ipa) audit and what were the results?

1150. Are there complementary rules to be used and are they applied?

1151. Did the additional works introduce minor or non-substantial changes to performance, as described in the contract documents?

1152. In case of decisions not to conclude a procurement or award a contract, were tenderers informed in writing and on a timely basis of the already stated decisions and grounds?

1153. Are there appropriate controls in place to ensure that procurement complies with the relevant legislation?

1154. Is there a general policy on approval of purchases?

1155. Is the performance of the procurement function/unit regularly evaluated?

1156. Are there reasonable procedures to identify possible sources of supply?

1157. If an order is divided among several vendors, is the explanation for that procedure documented?

1158. Does the procurement function/unit have the ability to secure best performance from contractors?

1159. Is there time waste during tendering?

1160. Does the contract meet criteria of completeness

and consistency?

5.2 Contract Close-Out: EDR Privileged Access Management

1161. Was the contract sufficiently clear so as not to result in numerous disputes and misunderstandings?

1162. Was the contract type appropriate?

1163. What happens to the recipient of services?

1164. Parties: Authorized?

1165. How is the contracting office notified of the automatic contract close-out?

1166. What is capture management?

1167. Have all acceptance criteria been met prior to final payment to contractors?

1168. Change in circumstances?

1169. Change in attitude or behavior?

1170. How does it work?

1171. Have all contracts been completed?

1172. Are the signers the authorized officials?

1173. Change in knowledge?

1174. Was the contract complete without requiring

numerous changes and revisions?

1175. Parties: who is involved?

1176. Have all contracts been closed?

1177. Has each contract been audited to verify acceptance and delivery?

1178. How/when used ?

1179. Have all contract records been included in the EDR Privileged Access Management project archives?

5.3 Project or Phase Close-Out: EDR Privileged Access Management

1180. How much influence did the stakeholder have over others?

1181. What hierarchical authority does the stakeholder have in your organization?

1182. Planned remaining costs?

1183. Have business partners been involved extensively, and what data was required for them?

1184. Planned completion date?

1185. What was the preferred delivery mechanism?

1186. Can the lesson learned be replicated?

1187. What could have been improved?

1188. What is the information level of detail required for each stakeholder?

1189. Complete yes or no?

1190. What benefits or impacts does the stakeholder group expect to obtain as a result of the EDR Privileged Access Management project?

1191. What is a Risk?

1192. Does the lesson educate others to improve performance?

1193. What process was planned for managing issues/risks?

1194. Were risks identified and mitigated?

1195. Which changes might a stakeholder be required to make as a result of the EDR Privileged Access Management project?

1196. Who exerted influence that has positively affected or negatively impacted the EDR Privileged Access Management project?

1197. What are they?

5.4 Lessons Learned: EDR Privileged Access Management

1198. What other questions should you have asked?

1199. Were any objectives unmet?

1200. How effective were your functional specs?

1201. What is the growth stage of the organization?

1202. Did the EDR Privileged Access Management project management methodology work?

1203. What were the problems encountered in the EDR Privileged Access Management project-functional area relationship, why, and how could they be fixed?

1204. How effectively were issues resolved before escalation was necessary?

1205. Overall, how effective were the efforts to prepare you and your organization for the impact of the product/service of the EDR Privileged Access Management project?

1206. How effectively and timely was your organizational change impact identified and planned for?

1207. How many government and contractor personnel are authorized for the EDR Privileged

Access Management project?

1208. How clearly defined were the objectives for this EDR Privileged Access Management project?

1209. What would you approach differently next time?

1210. What skills are required for the task?

1211. How useful was the content of the training you received in preparation for the use of the product/service?

1212. How effective was the documentation that you received with the EDR Privileged Access Management project product/service?

1213. Who had fiscal authority to manage the funding for the EDR Privileged Access Management project, did that work?

1214. How clear were you on your role in the EDR Privileged Access Management project?

1215. How well defined were the acceptance criteria for EDR Privileged Access Management project deliverables?

Index

270

portfolio   120, 241
portray 66
position   193
positioned   181-182
positive   91, 127, 139, 238
positively   262
possible   49, 56, 63, 72, 83, 94, 109, 113, 148, 228, 235, 248,
257
potential   22, 48, 66, 82, 84, 86-87, 110, 123, 135, 154, 177,
197, 201-202, 207, 211, 240, 244
practical   64, 77, 82, 94, 220
practice   196, 205
practices   1, 12, 65, 86, 101-102, 137, 151, 178, 195, 252
precaution   1
precede   166
precludes   211
predicting   100
predictive   169
preferred   261
pre-filled   10
prepare   171, 189, 198, 263
prepared   212
preparing   176
present   103, 108, 125, 196, 215, 243
presented   26, 140
preserve   43
preserved   67
pressures   164
prevent   56, 150, 232
prevents   24
previous   38, 130, 187, 250
previously   201, 223
primary   50, 169
principles   178, 195, 212
printing   9
priorities   47, 49, 51, 58, 183
prioritize   191, 206
priority 50, 52, 161, 235
privacy   32
private 137

proper 96, 248
properly   12, 34, 41, 130, 144, 203, 244
property   228
proposals   102, 211
proposed   24, 56-57, 81, 84, 138-139, 145, 202, 216, 250-251,
254
Propriety   241
protect   65, 110
protected   67
protection   107
protests   211
proved252
provide   71, 116, 120-121, 133, 144, 155, 165, 174, 182, 249
provided   9, 14, 105, 134, 151, 211-212
provider   171
providers   90
provides   144, 163, 170
providing   96, 133
provision   195
public 137, 256
publisher   1
pulled 121
purchase   10, 12, 209
purchased   12
purchases   214, 257
purpose   2, 12, 121, 129, 169, 182, 226, 234-235, 237
purposes   131, 154, 177
pushing   120
qualified   40, 62-64, 70, 75, 209, 248
qualifies   66
qualify 58, 63, 70
qualities   28
quality 1, 4-6, 12, 25, 47, 50, 61, 66-67, 75, 84, 105, 120, 157-158,
180, 183, 185, 187-190, 193-194, 196, 213, 227-229, 248
quantified   101
quantify   58
question   13-14, 18, 30, 46, 60, 77, 94, 107, 111, 189
questions   8, 10, 13, 64, 173, 238, 263
quickly 13, 62, 73, 75, 179
radically   60
raised 148
rather 109
rating 221

research   27, 107, 120, 148, 163, 228
reserve 154
reserved   1
reserves   191, 213
reside 79, 211
resistance   215
resolution   71, 92, 149
resolve 19-20, 23, 231, 234
resolved   187, 238, 263
resource   4-5, 119, 136, 155, 157, 167, 169-170, 195, 220
resources   2, 10, 21, 24-25, 27, 37, 40, 52, 69, 79, 95, 113,
117-118, 120, 131, 135, 137, 142, 151, 160-162, 169, 174, 179, 181,
196, 215, 230, 239, 243
respect 1
respond 136
responded   14
responding   201
response   27, 95, 100-101, 250
responses   78, 202, 211-212
responsive   174, 181
restrict 145
result   67, 79, 91, 149, 181, 183, 223, 242, 259, 261-262
resulted   99
resulting   74, 139
results 10, 34, 39, 65, 77, 80-81, 83-84, 86, 88, 90, 97, 105, 130,
136-137, 162, 172, 181, 186-187, 236, 245, 249, 253, 257
Retain 107
retained   70
retention   52
retrospect   121
return 91, 126, 190
revenue 18, 56
revenues   50
review 12-13, 41, 70, 139, 165, 176, 179, 201, 225
reviewed   40, 195
reviews12, 141, 172, 200, 213, 237, 245
revised 61, 99, 207
revisions   260
reward 55-56, 65, 220
rewarded   21
rewards 102
rework 50, 52, 185
rights 1

CPSIA information can be obtained
at www.ICGtesting.com
Printed in the USA
BVHW081415250719
554363BV00016B/1546/P

9 780655 821960